The
Heart of a
Good ♡ Thing

The *Heart* of a Good Thing

Beyond Destructive Patterns of History
Re*Discover*, Re*Vive*, Re*Ignite* & Re*Store*
New Beginnings of Bold Love in Your Relationships and Marriage

—— ANDREA BOWEYA ——

CONCLUSIO
HOUSE PUBLISHING

"*The Heart of a Good Thing* is exceptional at bringing clarity and simplicity to complex concerns."
-Lady Korrie

"I really hold on to what *The Heart of a Good Thing* says about willingness. I believe that nothing can be fully attained if we are not willing; and for many of us, it's an achievement in itself. Maladaptive interruptions—this is incredible! Such interruptions are very real. *The Heart of a Good Thing* has given me tangible things to hold on to." - Lady Shawnita

"For me, *The Heart of a Good Thing* is God's designed solution for restoration and new beginnings in relationship. It's a masterpiece for implementing God's redemptive plan." -Lady Marva

"God's original intent experienced and expressed! Lady Andrea, you captured this fully here" -Lady Cheryl

"*The Heart of a Good Thing* is like a relational time travel machine. It has helped me to revisit my past relational definition, rediscover my present definition and reignite possibilities with hope and great anticipation for the future." -Lady Jackie

*"**The Heart of a Good Thing** has reminded me to focus on the potential of what marriage can be when we reignite vision and passion."* -Lady Michelle

*"**The Heart of a Good Thing** really helped me to answer the what, why, and how of relationship and spirituality."* Lady Febbie

*"**Strengthen What Remains in The Heart of a Good** Thing really ministered to me. I am going to be bold about celebrating my marriage with no apologies."* -Lady Barbara

*"**The Heart of a Good Thing** has really encouraged me to never underestimate myself, but to know the full potential that God has given me."* -Lord Dimitri

"The Heart of a Good Thing"
REL012050 RELIGION / Christian Life / Love & Marriage
REL012130 RELIGION / Christian Life / Women's Issues

Printed in Canada
First Printing, 2018

ISBN 978-1-988847-04-7

Published by:
Conclusio House Publishing
Brampton, Ontario
Canada

www.conclusiohouse.com

Have you ever imagined who you would be if who you were created to be was never interrupted?

What if I tell you that you have a limitless source within to fully restore what God intended from the beginning?

One step at time, let's intentionally tap into this limitless source within, and live our full potential of bold love in relationship with self, others, and, ultimately, in marriage.

❤

The Heart of a Good Thing

Dedication

I owe so much of who I am to my grandmother—
"Mother"—Letitia Rebecca Jackson. This remarkable
wife and mother of fifteen children lived to one hundred
years young, and has taught me some of the most
valuable lessons about life and relationship that I have
come to hold dear.

When I was a baby, I struggled with an illness
that, among other things, robbed me of my audible
voice. Mother would tell me the story that, unlike most
children, I was void of the ability to at least cry when
in need. It genuinely grieved family members to look at
me, as I was very frail and lacking in appeal. My aunts
explain, though, that Mother had a knack for seeing way
beyond my appearance. She was so intentional about
being present and attentive to me that while very little
sound came from my body, what I was unable to voice
never really went unheard. Mother truly listened from
within, far beyond the capacity of her outer ears.

As I make meaning of this story throughout my life,
I have come to understand that Mother intentionally
became my audible voice when I didn't have such a voice.
She was able to hear my needs, far beyond my silence.
At a time when illness was most obvious in my life, she

focused on the possibility of my healing, instead. In my then broken capacity, she saw my full potential. I am so grateful that, from a tender age, Mother intentionally modelled for me the heart of relationship, what it means to discern the real depth of the inner voice, and how to truly listen, from such a sacred space, to the seemingly voiceless.

Mother taught me that

- ❤Silence does not mean there is no voice

- ❤Everyone and everything has a voice with an important story to share

- ❤Listening goes far beyond what you can audibly hear; therefore, it is important that you attentively listen beyond the capacity of your outer ear

- ❤When you carefully push past the barriers you see on the surface, you will find that beyond every obvious dis-ease and struggle lies a heart that simply longs to be loved. Love is ultimately what that heart needs to regain its full potential.

- ❤Love, demonstrated through intentional presence, is a key that unlocks healing in times of suffering

As a wife, Mother taught me that

- ❤Every woman has a particular gift that is able to transform what seems like nothing into something

❤ When a woman's heart is connected to the right man, it opens up invaluable possibilities for generations to come.

I am forever grateful for Mother's generational legacy of love that continues to fuel a deep life force in me each day. This legacy awakens a perpetual voice within me that echoes the endless possibilities of what love can bring to life, far beyond what seems impossible, in every destined relationship.

A Passed-on Legacy Word to You

The last time I had the honour of being with Mother on her one-hundredth birthday, she summoned me to sit with her. In that moment, she laid her hand on me with utmost love and declared that I was "carrying water." Right then and there, as if a halo was raised on my head, I realized why I was repeatedly led to read this one particular scripture leading up to my visit with Mother.

"I will rejoice over Jerusalem and be delighted with my people. There will never again be heard in that city the sounds of crying and sadness. There will never be a baby from that city who lives only a few days. And there will never be an older person who doesn't have a long life. A person who lives a hundred years will be called young…"
(Isaiah 65:19–20 NCV)

Here I was, absolutely stunned at realizing that I was right then being a witness to the tangible manifestation of this promised blessing. At one-hundred years young, Mother was, once again, attuned to the silent voice of the unborn then within me. From an internal place that was marked by previous struggle and uncertainty, she, in that moment, gave voice to a life-awakening force instead. This was July 2015. Mother Letitia went on to be with the Lord August 2015, just a few weeks later. The baby she spoke to in the womb was then born December 2015. Her name is now Letitia. I am convinced that God's tangible declaration and generational gift of promised restoration will continue, just like the one made possible through this incredible relationship continuum.

"Can these bones live? ... Prophesy to these bones, and say to them, 'O dry bones, hear the word of the Lord! Thus says the Lord God to these bones: 'Surely I will cause breath to enter into you, and you shall live."
(Ezekiel 37:3–5 NKJV)

I now share this same blessing of promised restoration and new beginning with you today. I declare that the seed of God's original intention in you will awaken in your heart, again. This good news will activate increased capacity in you to strengthen what remains. You will be summoned by the truth of God's Word and the truth of who you are apart from every negative interruption of the past. I declare that you will, again, know the life-awakening force that is able to restore each destined relationship that was once marked by sadness, dry bones, or crying. You will be strong enough to withstand any destructive lures of the past. You will instead experience the joy of love and loving in your life, your relationships, your marriage, and for generations to come. You are blessed to live a legacy of bold love. In Jesus' name, it is so.

Acknowledgements

Every day I grow more thankful to God for my extended family and, particularly, the men in my life who continue to help me believe that good things are possible. The ones who, no matter how far our culture may have swayed from a hopeful perspective of men, continue to remind me that great men do exist. Not without struggles and pains of their own, they willingly embrace the call to be great leaders and men of responsibility. They have opened some of the richest opportunities for me to grow, learn, heal, hope, serve, and *rediscover* our great strengths, apart from any historical, destructive patterns.

To my gift of responsibility, my best friend, and truly faith-filled husband, who asked me to marry him just two weeks after our first meeting; to the one who continues to boldly love, cover, coach, and launch me forward, Mr. Dimitri Ngombo Boweya. I am so grateful to God to have been chosen to carry your dimensional seed to life. I deeply respect and admire your leadership, through thick and thin. You are a genuine heart of *MANaging a Good Thing*.

To my father, Mr. Everton L. Jackson, the one who chose me, the uncle who has become my extraordinary father. Your selflessness, together with Mom and your unconditional love, has taught me that greater is indeed possible. You continue to teach me that one decision, one word, one genuine gift can transform an entire lifetime.

Dad, thank you for igniting the dreamer in me. I am forever grateful that you chose me.

To *The Restoration of Fatherhood* and *Legacy Moments* team that has braved this incredible dialogue-to-action movement with me for the past five years. Your commitment to rediscovering the true strength in every man and the collective strength in who we are together has been nothing short of phenomenal. Together, we have journeyed in carrying this seed to life, and have truly established a precedent, a great dimensional standard for ongoing restoration.

To every individual, couple, and family whom I have been privileged to counsel, you continue to teach me that restoring the health of the heart is our greatest priority. I am forever grateful that you have shared with me the honour of journeying with you. Thank you for continuing to teach me, every day, about the power of community. Your story is our story. Your courage to reach for healing and new beginnings is our journey. One moment at a time, one person at a time, one relationship at a time, we will chart an intentional pathway of possibilities for generations to come. It is possible.

Table of Contents

Step 4 -Re*Ignite* 99

Step 5 - Re*Store* 114

Foreword

The law of debit and credit is universal and runs through every aspect of life. All you need to do is observe, learn, and practise. *The Heart of a Good Thing* recognizes these two life lessons, and offers advice from the viewpoint of a clear understanding of both. It has healing elements, restorative panacea, formative guidelines, and expressive catholicon, all for relationships at all stages. To be honest, I wouldn't have expected less from Andrea.

I have come to know the Boweyas well. We got together with this family a little over five years ago, but we feel as though we have been one family all our lives. No one can ask for a better brother and sister from a different mother. The most striking thing about Andrea and Dimitri is that they continuously challenge my wife and me, and I believe every other couple who is in touch with them, with their dedication to making their love shine to all who are watching them; and in a deliberate way, that does not rob their bold love in anyone's face. They are just a beautiful couple to watch. It seems to me that what we share in common most is our passion for spending the better part of our ministry lives helping relationships, marriages, good-personhood, and the creation of great young families. In my case, I have discovered that we can never do too much in this area. The need increases daily. It, therefore, gives me exceptional joy to see more efforts geared towards this noble cause.

When I got this book, I thought of Victor Hugo's declaration that "There is only one thing stronger than all armies in the world, and that is an idea whose time has come." *The Heart of a Good Thing* is perfect for this moment. It is the time for this idea, in this moment. God values relationships beyond what we have been able to imagine, and that explains why He said in Genesis 2:18, *"It is not good that the man should be alone."* If God says it is not good, then it is simply not good anytime, which is why it is important to rediscover, revive, reignite, and restore at every stage of life and relationship. It does not matter one's age.

Negative focus creates blindness. Unfortunately, the human race has completely redefined relationship, and, in so doing, has inverted the original design concept. The bigger issue arising from this distortion is that people deliberately forget the fact that this *focus creates blindness*. When you focus on the negative, you become blind to the positive. When you are not crediting any part of your life, you are simply debiting it, and this is most true in relationships, especially marriages. The media, internet, social media, idea marketers, even writers and celebrities have all pulled most people's focus towards the negatives. So we tend to be totally blind to the positives. The problem, therefore, is our focus. Men and women spend all their awake hours looking for what their partners did wrong, what they are doing wrong, and what they will do wrong. The same attitude gets carried to work, to church, to associations, and even to national and global forums. *The Heart of a Good Thing* invites you to spend those hours asking, "What about the things they did right?" "What about the things they are doing right?" and "What about the things they will do right?"

This book did not stop there. It provides five broad steps and breaks down those steps into daily practices. In my opinion, this is a big step towards building a great next generation. Andrea writes in a simple, easy-to-read style, yet her arrangement of the steps is systematic, with excellent flow. The greater beauty about the five steps is that you can either work with the whole package, or select the part that addresses where you are right now and go straight there to get your own action plans on practicing that part of your *heart of a good thing*. It makes you intentional. Try to get a check-up, you might need a heart check, a rediscovery, a revival, a reigniting, or a restoration. Whichever one, or set, you need, *The Heart of a Good Thing* gives some great steps to take. I recommend it. I really do. And I applaud the on-time idea.

Pastor Chris Chukwuma
Pre-Marital and Marriage Counselling Ministries

Preface

In my almost twenty years of journeying with individuals, couples, and families as a psychotherapist, I have come to understand that in life painful things can, and do, happen. Such experiences are almost always connected to meaningful relationships. Whether reinforced through historical patterns, culture, family of origin, or other individuals, these ordeals injure us deeply and interrupt our identity or who we were created to be in the beginning. Both consciously and unconsciously, negative experiences of the past distort the truth about who we are as individuals, and further contribute to an accumulation of negative perspectives in the way we do relationship. I have also learned over the years that while painful experiences are deeply damaging, it is what happens next that really defines our ultimate perspective in life and the path we then take in relationship, with ourselves, with others, and, ultimately, in marriage. We have all fallen or been hurt at one time or another. It is not so much the fall or hurt that defines who you are or your capacity for relationship, but rather how you have been restored, or not, towards getting up again. "*For the lovers of God may suffer adversity and stumble seven times, but they will continue to rise over and over again...*" (Proverbs

24:16 TPT). An intentional journey of rising beyond the past to restore new beginnings—whether by letting go of abusive situations or working harder at destined ones—is what defines our outcome and experience of relationship.

Every moment after the pain, the trauma, or the dysfunction of our collective past signals a need for restoration. There is a need to repair what was/is broken. When this need remains unmet, it limits our love capacity, and destructive patterns are created and sustained, instead. The truth is, your heart was fully wired, from the beginning, for genuine love and relationship. This is God's intention and design. Yet for many, this full potential has been so interrupted that we have been blocked from what was always intended. We have lived with a silent yet loud inner tension. On one hand, there is a spiritual invitation to be where we were designed to be, but on the other hand, there is a counter-pull to maintain a familiar, yet less-than-full potential or broken capacity.

Awareness Is Key

Whether the journey is about healing from the pain of the past or changing the patterns of history or raising the standard of love we now live, the missing link is often awareness. An awareness nudge is needed to bring us back to who we truly are, and from where we are to where God intended for us to be. As a collective, we have struggled to understand our identity and have come to accept a life in relationship with self, others, and our spouse that is way less than our full-potential capacity. Over time, we have grown used to being okay with what's not okay. Abnormal patterns of the past have also existed so long that they have unwittingly become accepted as the norm. Intentional rediscovery towards restoration is crucial. It is the key when the goal is to successfully live in the full strength of love that God intended, Christ redeemed, and that is really needed in our relationship experience today.

A relationship that mirrors Christ and bold love is God's design and the experience that everyone deserves to live. After all that "should not have been," we are now called by God to have a heart check-up to rediscover, revive, reignite, and restore what was always meant to be. It is a process that will lead us to be healed, bold, and purposeful in relationship with self, others, and our spouse, again. It is a process that will lead us to being safe enough to experience a needed sense of belonging again, and live from a place of true identity, again.

The voice of restoration says, "You are not alone. I am here with you. I am invested in you. Far beyond what seems like limited or broken capacity, I believe in you. I believe in your ability to access and live from the full potential that God has given you." Restoration says, "I will open doors of possibilities with you for new beginnings of greater love. It is possible!"

A Journey of Possibilities

About six years ago, God stirred my heart from this place of possibilities to publish my first book, *Legacy Moments*. I was moved by a goal to shift the disconnected generational reality that I saw, so often, at the heart of present relationship injuries and destructive patterns.

Legacy Moments became a practical tool to support individuals and families in correcting this generational gap, by intentionally rethinking and recording a God-given legacy and providing a clear path for generations to come. One year later, together with a phenomenal team, we began what we called a dialogue-to-action conference—"The Restoration of Fatherhood." When I initially received what I believe was a God-instruction to begin hosting such a gathering, I must admit that I questioned my capacity. I said to myself, actually to God, "But I'm a woman." I saw my own limitations, but I said "Yes," anyway. Far beyond my imagination, five years later and from one brave "It is possible," The Restoration of Fatherhood became an incredible place of restoring honour and affirmation to so many men, women, and families. As a collective, men embraced a sense of safety in being vulnerable and built up, as we hailed them for who they were, rather than focus on or bash them for what they lacked. Women collectively moved beyond a place of just a dream to an increasingly secure place of being covered by the men in their lives. This was a God move by far.

So as my heart was again stirred by a God-instruction to write *The Heart of a Good Thing*, I said, "Yes!" Without focusing on any limitation that came to mind, I now saw something wonderful. Reaching back to Mother's blessing, there was a confident echo inside of me that said, "It is possible." It was only then, and after I initiated the process of writing, that God allowed me to realize that all along The Restoration of Fatherhood was precisely initiated by Him as a key to *The Heart of a Good Thing*. Right, first things first.

"Beloved children, our love can't be an abstract theory we only talk about, but a way of life demonstrated though loving deeds" (1 John 3:18 TPT).

As I continue to sit with individuals and couples each day in the safety of a counselling space, I hold to this truth that restoring bold love through God's design and intention for relationship is indeed possible. I have seen how this intentional belief and ongoing action have literally changed the negative trajectory of destructive patterns, proving again and again that beyond the deepest pains of the past, it is possible to restore the heart through love. I write from this place of truth. I write to remind myself, as well as you, that one moment at a time, one person at a time, one marriage at a time, restoration, and greater in new beginnings, is possible. I prophesy to you that there is an open heaven in this season for the restoration of divinely intended relationships and marriages back to a place of bold, full potential in God. One intentional step at a time, it is possible.

I am deeply convinced that far beyond what we could imagine, you and I have the depth of strength and resilience needed to open up such doors of possibilities to love as God intended. *The Heart of a Good Thing* will empower you to live in relationship with self, others, and, ultimately, with your spouse in this place of possibilities and full potential, as God intended. Beyond every maladaptive interruption and destructive pattern of the past, *The Heart of a Good Thing* will support you to restore a corrective paradigm of bold love through five spiritually infused practical steps:

Step 1: A Heart Check-Up—an ongoing invitation to safe willingness of heart. Be willing to do the work.

Step 2: ReDiscover who you are—your identity, purpose, and role, as God intended, apart from every maladaptive interruption.

Step 3: ReVive what your heart, and the heart or your relationship, really needs. ReVive your heartbeat, by discerning and investigating the interruptions and blockages, and regaining what the heart needs: love.

Step 4: ReIgnite—awaken passion and vision, again, to love beyond limits. Reignite your ability to see great possibilities and new beginnings.

Step 5: ReStore boldness in love, every day, through L.O.V.E., and bring back what was truly intended and is needed. Revolutionize your relationships and marriage for generations to come.

Take each step intentionally, one at a time, or go where you most need to begin. Your life in love and relationship will never be the same again. You will transform pain into healing and pass into a future of new beginnings. What was business as usual will now become the incredible wealth of *bold love* as intended. Remember wealth untapped becomes poverty, but love unblocked becomes the true wealth you and I most need. It is possible!

With love,

Andrea Boweya

Introduction

If you are like me, you have had the experience of being out to eat with a friend or colleague. You thought about the limits in your budget and ordered accordingly, even though you secretly wanted something better. By the end of the meal, your friend or colleague reaches for the bill and says, "I got it. I have enough." "Oh my goodness," you think to yourself, "I could have actually had the better, yet more expensive, thing I really wanted."

"Now faith brings our hopes into reality and becomes the foundation needed to acquire the things we long for" (Hebrews 11:1 TPT).

Someone has already invested all they have just so you could choose, beyond hope, to have the best of what your heart longs for in your life, relationships, or marriage. Beyond the great heroes of faith in the past who hoped but did not obtain evidence of the promise. *"Now God has invited us to live in something better than what they had — faith's fullness! This is so that they [the promise] could be brought to finished perfection alongside of us"* (Hebrews 11:40 TPT). This is a promised blessing for your life and relationship. God Himself has forever been at the beginning and end of every experience in your life as the one saying, "I got it. I have enough." You really have the opportunity to choose better instead, through Him who continues to be the giver of all good and perfect gifts (James 1:17). Sometimes, however, to no fault of our own, we choose way less than He continues to offer, because we have unwittingly come to believe, deep inside, that we deserve less. I want to remind you that God knows your needs, and as the ultimate lover of your soul, has literally given all just so you can see that you are worth faith's fullness in love and relationship. *"For this is how much God loved the world – he gave his one and only, unique Son as a gift. So now everyone who believes in him will never perish but experience everlasting life"* (John 3:16 TPT). Does your heart perceive it?

From a beginning that was messed up by the first Adam, God went all out and gave us Jesus as a second beginning from Adam, so that better could be made perfect. Beyond the reality of pain, a good relationship could be made better, and better could be made perfect through the gift of love that God gave. God's love is the greatest sacrifice and model for relationship, to ensure you and I have the best pattern and potential to also correct any messed-up-relationship reality. From the Garden of Eden and now through the Garden of Gethsemane, Jesus came and gave Himself fully so that, through Him, we could redeem what was lost and instead restore the promise of "in the beginning" and so that it could be brought to finished perfection alongside us (Hebrews 11:40). That's just amazing. This is *The Heart of a Good Thing*. The key is bold love.

Never in history has it been more important than it is

right now for you and me to make an intentional choice to restore God's intention in the way we live and display relationship and marriage. This is crucial, because with the passing of time, our collective reality, practice, and experience of love and relationship has progressively dwindled. A sense of security in community has also been diminished. For many, a less-than-better reality continues to be the inadvertent experience. All the while, if we are able to see it, we yet have full access to love boldly through this treasure that is in us as earthen vessels (2 Corinthians 4:6–9). We have the ability to make known the excellence of God through the way we love in our relationships.

Relationship Is One of God's Greatest Gifts to Humanity.

Relationship is a genuine need. It is a deep desire in all of our hearts. In spite of all the "in spite of's," relationship intrigues us. It draws us in. We learn to build safe connection with some, draw away from others, try again, and even bring some to a close, which is okay, especially when it wasn't God intended. Yet relationship remains a key factor in our present and future success. Since the beginning of time, relationship has been a continuum that moves us through every stage of life. It is the currency of human development and the source of every new beginning. We never outgrow our need for love and relationship, which requires us to continually embrace new beginnings. When we truly desire the best of new beginnings, it is also important to create space in our hearts by addressing any destructive patterns of the past that may have taken the place of what was intended. It is important for us to know what we are working with, so that the work can be most precise and effective. In counselling language, we say, "Assessment before intervention."

I am aware that the journey towards new beginnings and better can sometimes seem complicated. After all, we have lived through an entire history of challenges. However, think about it in this simplified way: When the abnormal takes the place of what God intended, a divine gift and vital need remains entrapped. The generational flow of love and relationship also continues to be distorted, devalued, and even missing in our ongoing legacy. So let's make one deliberate choice. Let's boldly do what is indeed possible to ultimately restore the heart of what was originally designed and needed. What we need more of is love.

What I do know from my own life, and from journeying with so many, is that beyond the seemingly automatic descent of historically negative experiences in our lives, there is also a God-given depth of wealth in all of us that yet remains from the beginning blessing—be fruitful in love and multiply in love. I have seen, time and time again, how when this wealth is rediscovered it becomes such an anchor for us, beyond where we have been to a place of life-giving love and new beginnings. When we become aware enough and willing enough to do a *heart check-up* to *rediscover, revive, reignite,* and *restore* such a potential, a legacy of bold love will become an incredible reality today and a clear relationship pathway for generations to come. *The Heart of a Good Thing* will guide you to intentionally restore and live the kind of bold love that was intended from the beginning.

In The Beginning

A Biblical Narrative

❤

"Then God said, 'Let Us make man in Our image, according to Our likeness'… So God created man in His own image; in the image of God He created him; male and female He created them. Then God blessed them, and God said to them, 'Be fruitful and multiply; fill the earth and subdue it'…Then God saw everything that He had made, and indeed it was very good."
(Genesis 1:26–28; 31)

Through the scriptural narrative of Genesis 1–3, it is clear that the evolution of time is intricately connected to the evolution of humanity in relationship. This process or continuum begins and spans from the biblical story of creation and birth as we see it today. The continuum of relationship moves us through life from birth to various life relationships and, ultimately, to intended marriage, where creation or birth is then, again and again, initiated. In generational succession, therefore, today's man and woman are, in essence, a continuum of relationship from the historical man and woman of yesterday. While we are each unique in some ways, we are also a remnant of what we will refer to as the historical man and historical woman.

There are two biblical streams of this relationship continuum. The first stream began with God's creation of the first man and woman, in relationship with Himself and with each other, from the DNA or likeness of God Himself. They were created with the full potential for love. I call this a paradigm of bold love. This is key to *the heart of a good thing.*

The second stream also began with the story of Adam and Eve, but from a place of unfaithfulness to the "in the beginning" stream and resulting destructive patterns, counter to what God intended for relationship and marriage. I call this a paradigm of maladaptive interruptions.

Before every other beginning, you and I had the purest first beginning in God. Whenever the journey of life interrupts this first beginning, the heart of God is always there, willing and ready to bring us back to the start, again. He holds this spiritual initiative faithfully, and gives us scriptures to believe and action this into reality.

"You formed my innermost being, shaping my delicate inside and my intricate outside, and wove them all together in my mother's womb. I thank you, God, for

making me so mysteriously complex! Everything you do is marvelously breathtaking. It simply amazes me to think about it! How thoroughly you know me, Lord! You even formed every bone in my body when you created me in the secret place, carefully, skillfully shaping me from nothing to something. You saw who you created me to be before I became me! Before I'd ever seen the light of day, the number of days you planned for me were already recorded in your book" (Psalm 139:13-16 TPT).

You were created and skillfully shaped, in your innermost being, by Love to love. To love is your utmost priority in life and relationship. To love the Lord with all your heart, soul and mind; and to love your neighbor as yourself is the first and greatest commandment that God gave to us from the beginning (Matthew 22:37). One step at a time, let's journey back to this beginning.

A Paradigm of Bold Love:
The Key to the Heart of a Good Thing

Relationship is currency. The more deeply rooted it is in God, the more wealth it produces. I believe that the story about God's creation of the first man and woman was intended to represent the deep essence of an "in the beginning," uninterrupted-relationship reality. It was a relationship that was fuelled by a currency system of love and the heart of just what God intended. Like every good relationship today, the key factor was that this relationship began from God's initiative. When God initiates a relationship, He says it is good. There was also ongoing and uninterrupted communication with God, and this God-human connection was the main source of life's decision making.

This "in the beginning" model was intended to be the foundation for every relationship, both then and today. From birth to marriage, the initiative and instruction of God is the most important foundation for sustainable generational success in relationship. This first continuum stream as a paradigm of bold love is, therefore, a spiritual initiative, yet a very practical endeavour. God created, instructed, and then gave us the responsibility to implement, without interruption, what was created and instructed.

Relationship is currency. The more deeply rooted it is in God, the more wealth it produces.

Can you imagine? What if you had no interruptions at all in your understanding of who you truly are, and engaged in relationship with your fullest potential, as originally intended? I believe that it was this God-identity factor and full potential that lent to a bold reality of self-acceptance and demonstrated non-judgment in love in the beginning. This level of awareness, in what was the first sacred space, showed that even the nakedness (the stuff) of the man and woman was no occasion for either to be ashamed. This was because their covering was first a spiritual initiative, and in principle this superseded every mentally and physically distracting thing. That's phenomenal!

A Paradigm of Bold Love

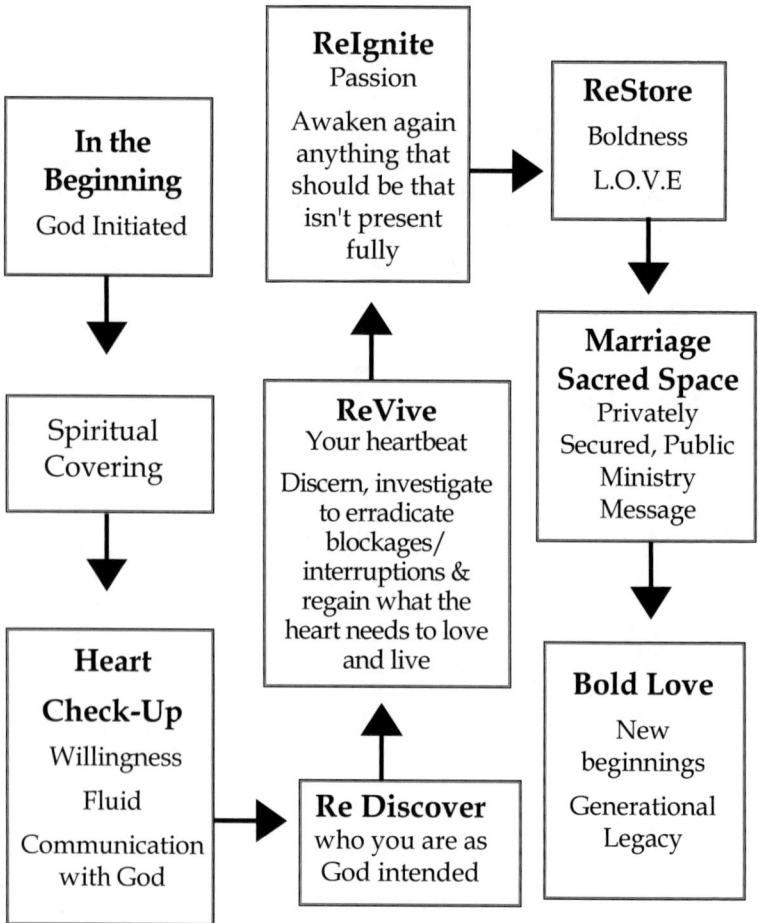

ReIgnite
Passion

Awaken again anything that should be that isn't present fully

ReStore
Boldness
L.O.V.E

In the Beginning
God Initiated

ReVive
Your heartbeat

Discern, investigate to erradicate blockages/ interruptions & regain what the heart needs to love and live

Marriage Sacred Space
Privately Secured, Public Ministry Message

Spiritual Covering

Heart Check-Up
Willingness
Fluid
Communication with God

Re Discover
who you are as God intended

Bold Love
New beginnings
Generational Legacy

In the Beginning:

A Natural Heritage Narrative

"But you must continue in the things which you have learned and been assured of, knowing from whom you have learned them, and that from childhood you have known the Holy Scriptures, which are able to make you wise for salvation through faith which is in Christ Jesus."(2 Timothy 3:14-15)

A few months before this book was published, I invited a group of amazing women to join me for a pre-launch. As I shared the contents of the book with them, we engaged in a great conversation. One of the things that really stood out to me was the many reminders that we, in fact, have a rich "in the beginning" natural heritage, however one we have swayed from. There is much to reach back to from our natural beginning story in relationship, while acknowledging as well how far we have come from "in the beginning." Let me list a few points that may refresh your own memory of a least interrupted beginning way back in history, if it *rings a bell* just say, "Ah ha":

- Life was lived in slow motion, compared to the busyness of today

- Family was community, and community was family. There was a strong sense of belonging. No appointment was needed to visit anyone in the community

- Everyone knew how to make or fix something; you could build or repair a whole house from close-to-home expertise, just for the price of genuine relationship. Sharing resources was second nature

- Spiritual instruction and the things of God were treated with utmost reverence and intensity. Plan B was seldom even acknowledged as an option

- Good testimonies were loud and common. There was even a weekly service scheduled just for this. It was not uncommon for someone to testify saying that they prayed for something because they had a need, then in no time a neighbour would arrive at the door, delivering enough to meet that need. There was a connection way beyond just natural interaction

- Parents really owned the responsibility to guide the path for their children's success as a unified goal together with the community

- Parents were present and purposeful in their

attention to family. This was the norm

- Routine meals with family were commonplace. It wasn't fast food — well, they were hardly present then

- Actually, "food" meant "ground provision" or what you pick from your tree or reaped from your garden — okay, this really shows where I began ☺

- Education was a priority

- School and community were trusted to be on the same level as parents in instruction and discipline. Sometimes the aunty was even the teacher. School was driven by loyalty to the success of the community

- Marriage was really celebrated and prepared for from a young age; non-marital intimate relationship was far from the norm back then

- When women gave birth, it was from a standing or squatting position; the nature of gravity was the intervention. The elders were the attending nurses

- Birthing and naming traditions were cause for great celebration

- Knowledge and application of natural medicine was beyond phenomenal; just a bush in the yard was all it took to heal the worst disease. The elders were beyond world class in there medicinal expertise

- Being an Elder meant that you were a genuine leader. The focus was to maintain health and growth in the community at large

- Photos were black and white, and they were printed to show. There were no lost photos because of lost phones

- There was very little technology, and very little interruption to needed connection and face-to-face conversation. Pen-pals rocked!

- In summary, relationship was needed to the same degree that it is needed now, but relationship was prioritized and practised more back then in our natural history.

There is great wisdom in 2 Timothy 3:14–15 that is applicable to all of life. Both with the spiritual things and the natural ones as well, *"continue in such things that you have learned, knowing from whom you have learned them."* This doesn't mean that you move to the country, so that you can plant and reap "food" from your own garden. Just being aware of what was interrupted in principle, but authentically good, is what's needed. Looking back at your own natural heritage narrative, or even remnants of your uninterrupted history, has the potential to make you wiser in your everyday relationship decision making. When you look back, what do you see?

A Paradigm of Maladaptive Interruptions: Unfaithfulness

"Now the serpent was more cunning than any beast of the field which the Lord God had made. And he said to the woman, 'Has God indeed said, You shall not eat of every tree of the garden?' So when the woman saw that the tree was good for food, that it was pleasant to the eyes, and a tree desirable to make one wise, she took of its fruit and ate. She also gave to her husband with her, and he ate. Then the eyes of both of them were opened, and they knew that they were naked; and they sewed fig leaves together and made themselves coverings."
(Genesis 3:1, 6–7)

A second stream in the continuum of relationship was initiated in Genesis 3:1–7. Here, a counter-model of the "in the beginning" historical man and woman began. This second stream was initiated by what I call the first maladaptive interruption in time, which then created a new opposing relationship paradigm. A maladaptive interruption is any event, experience, or resulting belief system that serves to distort or ultimately destroy God's original intention for who you are as a person and the full potential of who you were designed to be in relationship with others.

Maladaptive interruptions are often historical, cultural, or psychological in nature, with a chief characteristic of infringing unwittingly, yet deeply rooted, destructive patterns in our perception of self—your identity and behaviour in relationship. They are the *stuff* that often silences our voice and robs us of our identity and sense of power within. We will explore the reality of some common maladaptive interruptions and their far-reaching negative effects in the next chapter.

The Bible gives a good view of the root and intention of maladaptive interruptions in John 10:10. The initiator here sees your worth and is aware of the wealth in your original identity. With a goal to steal, kill, and destroy your full potential, he intervenes by first challenging the voice of God in you and who you are through a maladaptive experience, historical event, or belief system. Remember, everyone and everything has a voice. Here, the voice of the resulting destructive pattern then becomes the loudest voice you hear, and lures you to accept a lesser view of who you are than what was intended by God. Your identity is then entrapped and your belief and behaviour in relationship with self and others becomes entrapped as well. All the while, God's gift for you remains that you would have life and love more abundantly, again.

Maladaptive interruptions are *crafty*, and unless discerned and correctively interrupted, they serve to distort your God-given identity and full potential. Beyond a one-time historical event or negative experience, the effects of maladaptive interruptions are maintained through destructive belief systems and behavioural patterns in a cycle of unfaithfulness to God's plan. Each time we see ourselves as less than God has created us to be, we unwittingly reinforce the harsh reality of this cycle and paradigm. A prevailing disconnected nature in families and culture is evidence.

Through maladaptive interruptions and our conscious or unconscious participation in a counter-path to God's original intention, a cycle of unfaithfulness in relationship, both spiritually and naturally, has continued through generations. Destructive patterns have been

A maladaptive interruption is any event, experience, or resulting belief system that serves to distort or ultimately destroy God's original intention for who you are as a person and the full potential of who you were designed to be in relationship with others.

repeated so much over time that the abnormal continues to take the place of the intended normal. Without full awareness, the ongoing negative impacts have become lodged in the way we do relationship, and incorporated as part of business as usual.

In the paradigm of maladaptive interruptions, the enemy assumes the place of God and, therefore, distorts the ultimate source of our identity and our full potential to do relationship from a place of bold love. Over time, limited capacity and a less-than-healthy reality in relationship is presumed as normal. Unwittingly accepting this abnormal structure as the norm has been at the heart of the greatest tragedy in relationship and marriage for many generations. This was also the reality initially seen in Genesis 3, when the enemy used a cunning lure to appeal to the psyche of this relationship. By interrupting the voice of God, and by human acceptance of this interruption as the norm, he ultimately led this relationship to a diminished place in spirit, mind, and body. The truth is, they were doing very well at the time and could have done better, but the opportunity for better was interrupted, and as this interruption was accepted, the relationship became far below what God intended. This maladaptive interruption truly attacked the very heartbeat of relationship and marriage to a diminished place of unfaithfulness, a reality that is still deeply experienced on many levels today. Their *stuff* now became the focus, instead of their strengths; they were now naked and ashamed.

Through, the first historical man and woman in Genesis 3, we see an initiated destructive pattern of blame, fault, judgment, and shame. This is one of the most identifiable hallmarks of the maladaptive interruption paradigm at work in relationships and marriages today. Godly identity was also distorted, and seeing ourselves less than our full potential ensued then. Our divine role, purpose, and empowered responsibility for desired change became displaced, all unwittingly in action while the hidden agenda remained mostly hidden from our conscious thinking. Sacred intimacy with God, and with each other, also became entrapped. From an intended high spiritual foundation, the historical man and woman were inadvertently shifted into a relationship that became physically and institutionally driven, instead. Do you see the resemblance today?

The historical man and woman, who were before familiar with unashamed, bold love, now struggled, like many today, with a loss of identity, wrestling in relationship from a limited physical disposition, resulting from distanced intimacy with God and a clear perspective of "in the beginning." It is a reality that is maintained, albeit often unconsciously, each time you accept the negative patterns of history or fail to prioritize the pattern of God's bold love in relationship. Without intentional awareness, to a large degree, the historical man, woman, and culture of today have continued to maintain a cycle of unfaithfulness by choosing less. A relationship reality that was meant to be a spiritual, mental, and physical union has, in many ways, become a maladaptive physical reality instead. This cycle of unfaithfulness continues to perpetuate a deeply broken system of relationship in hearts, families, and communities.

Maladaptive Interruption Paradigm

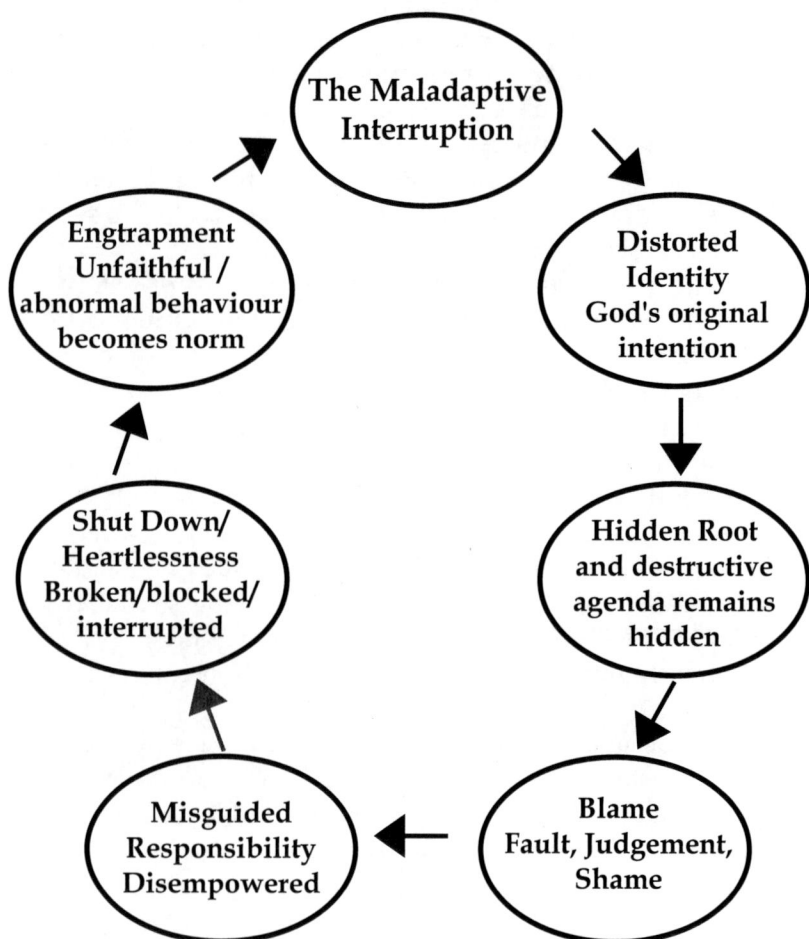

The Maladaptive Interruption

Distorted Identity
God's original intention

Hidden Root and destructive agenda remains hidden

Blame
Fault, Judgement, Shame

Misguided Responsibility
Disempowered

Shut Down/
Heartlessness
Broken/blocked/
interrupted

Engtrapment
Unfaithful /
abnormal behaviour
becomes norm

The Cycle of Maladaptive Interruptions

1. The Maladaptive Interruption — History, destructive patterns in culture and system of belief, experience of trauma, relationship injuries (Genesis 3:1–4).

2. Distorts your identity and God's original intention — Who you are, including the voice and God's intention for your life, is interrupted. From "I am wonderfully made" to "I am not good enough" (Genesis 3:6–11). *Corrective Interruption*: Become more aware of how past experiences have interrupted who you are as God created you to be.

3. Hidden root and destructive agenda remains hidden — On the surface, it may seem like a fight between you and someone else; however, the fight is actually between you and the spirit of the interruption. The destructive agenda to steal, kill, and destroy (Genesis 3:1; John 10:10) is often at the root of a surface fight, without awareness. *Corrective Interruption*: The truth makes us free. You have a limitless capacity to discern what's

deeper than the surface. You have the gift of bold love and abundant life as the right choice. Wrestling with flesh and blood, when the agenda is far beyond, only serves to maintain lack of awareness of the negative impact of the interruption, and limits God's intended mastery in you over this hidden root. Commit to seeing beyond before you love less or fight again (Ephesians 6:12–18). **Note:** These first three realities in the maladaptive paradigm are sometimes less obvious, yet they are often the most active underlying drivers to an ongoing maladaptive reality of pain in your relationship with self, others, and, ultimately, in marriage.

4. Blame, fault, judgment, and shame (Genesis 3:12–13; Romans 8:1–39) — Blame, fault, judgment, and resulting shame are often the most obvious evidence of a maladaptive interruption paradigm at work in a relationship. *Corrective Interruption*: Be less focused on being justified with such a response. Become more aware of the obvious blame, fault, or judgment as a pathway to see and challenge what is less obvious in points 1, 2, and 3. A predominant focus on blame, fault, judgment, and resulting shame further contributes to more counter intended outcomes, leading you onward to points 5, 6, and 7.

5. Misguided Responsibility (Romans 3:23; Galatians 6:5) — Here, focus is misguided. Blame, fault, judgment, and resulting shame from number 4 most often holds "the other" accountable for

change. There is a disconnection from your own innate power to initiate what you most need. In relationship, there is a lack of intended focus on the beginning vision or God's instructions. *Corrective Interruption*: While blaming the one who "should" be judged or held accountable may seem only fair or right, a predominant focus on blame is also a snare that keeps us blocked from what our heart truly needs — love, healing, growth, and new beginnings. It is important to know that the ones who *should* aren't often the ones who genuinely *could* offer what is truly needed, because of their own limited capacity. For example, expecting just that person to meet your need for an apology sometimes means that this need remains unmet if they lack the capacity. Be empowered to receive what you need from within.

6. Shut-down Heart/Heartlessness — *"Hope deferred makes the heart sick"* (Proverbs 13:12). When there is an ongoing progression from points 1 to 5 without corrective interruption, the heart remains broken and, without needed restoration, shuts down. Trust and openness to matters of the heart is withheld or diminished. Walls go up, which then blocks access to genuine awareness, healing, growth, and possibilities to love and be loved. *Corrective Interruption*: A heart check-up. Be willing to keep your heart alive and open to revive the flow of love.

7. Entrapment — Abnormal beliefs and destructive

behaviours are practiced over time and become unwittingly accepted as normal. Decisions are more often made apart from God's original intent. Maladaptive interruptions are then reinforced and demonstrated in relationship with self, others, and one's spouse, if not correctively interrupted. *Corrective Interruption*: Bold love — A Heart Check-Up, ReDiscover, ReVive, ReIgnite, and Restore.

The Reality of Maladaptive Interruptions

c——————— ♥ ———————ɔ

"Though the ropes of the wicked have ensnared me, I have not forgotten your instruction." (Psalm 119:61)

The life we live today in relationship is truly informed by the conscious and unconscious choices or experiences of our past. The events of history really do contribute to stereotypes. Every culture has had its own significant experiences of maladaptive interruptions that have affected systems of belief and behaviour on a wide scale. A commitment to knowing what and how experiences and culture have affected the way we do relationship is an important thing.

An Afro-Caribbean Awareness Perspective

Knowing the strengths of a culture is as important as understanding the struggles. If you are like me, as mentioned earlier, you may have grown up with a strong sense of community in a time when the wider community was like an extended family. Looking back, this sense of community seems, against odds, to have been least maladaptively interrupted from the past. The community was home. You may also relate to the strong sense of loyalty that existed in community, for better or for worse, both in holding honourable respect for each other and also in holding true to a sometimes negative culture of forbearance, maintaining a "what happens at home stays at home" expectation of silence. While we hold on to the strength of community, a culture of forbearance also has historically robbed us of this strength within. At the same time, it is undeniable that silence has also been a safe response to an ingrained culture of gossip.

The heart of Afro-centric music, then and now, has also been least interrupted. If like me you thoroughly enjoy African music, you will realize that there is a more consistent demonstrated oneness between music and the heart of the artist. You will see a picture, not of a person simply singing a song or doing a dance, but rather of a person literally being one with the song and the dance. If you haven't yet indulged, go ahead, watch and listen to some African music. Okay, maybe I'm projecting my taste for music onto you. But do you know that, beyond the surface, the authenticity of music in the African culture was historically less interrupted because it was deemed less of a threat in the economically driven exploitation of this culture? Music has, therefore, remained an

A commitment to knowing what and how experiences and culture have affected the way we do relationship is an important thing.

instrument of coping and healing in the face of grave pain. Music has also historically allowed individuals to rediscover access to their heart through this art. Psychologically, music further invites a deep sense of connection with God, self, and others. The next time you are present at a named Black church, just observe and say, "Ah ha," as you notice this to be true—a oneness with song or dance.

Slavery, on the other hand, was one of the most significant interruptions to the heart of family, marriage, and relationship. By far, this has been one of the most damaging maladaptive interruptions to an entire culture of rich traditions, and one which signalled a cycle of unfaithfulness.

Looking Back

Looking back, you may relate to the experience of growing up not knowing who was really married to whom. Or you may remember that intimacy appeared to be outlawed and forced to be hidden, where it was knowingly disrespectful to show genuine affection in public. Maybe you can relate to not being able to count how many individuals were faithfully married, but could easily count how many children in one "yard" carried different last names. Does the jeer of a "one burner" man mean anything to you? Or maybe you can relate to the unspoken "If you are a married man and you don't have a mistress, then something is wrong with you." Or maybe you may relate to being married and somehow knowing that your relationship mirrors more of a functional arrangement than the type of full love reality you dreamt of or expected.

Reflecting on the accumulative lessons from my faithful Black History class in high school, I will attempt to summarize some key conceptualizations of the similarities in the relationship patterns from then that are still collectively distinct today. While not from an entirely linear cause-and-effect perspective, by exploring the similarities between now and then, you may see how slavery has had a significant, lasting impact on the systems of family, relationship, and marriage, particularly in the Afro-Caribbean heritage.

If you are even vaguely aware, think back with me. As individuals were frequently transported from one place to another involuntarily, relationships, marriages, and families were separated without any real hope of reuniting. By function of its potentially distracting nature from economic gain, the bold demonstration of love was also generally prohibited. While the need for relationship and affection remained as it should, the proverbial object of affection was enslaved and often violated. Heart connections were severed without notice in order to meet plantation-driven goals. The heart and the needed continuum of relationship were debased. Because we never grow out of our need for love and relationship, an ongoing desire to meet this need was then directed to starting over and over again from a maladaptive perspective when heart connections were prematurely ended. Unfaithfulness to authentic values, traditions, and identity became the functional option; moving on abruptly without heart connections became the norm. What was once a system of authentic heart connections now became a pattern of just physical relations, instead. Remaining disconnected, shut down, or heartless seemed to make the inevitable, unannounced moving on from place to place easier than it would have otherwise been. In order to cope with what was insurmountable for the heart, the heart of the historical man and woman during slavery became progressively less involved. Do you see it? An extended practice of unfaithfulness or heartless connections counter to what God intended became the norm. This has been a deep and prevailing maladaptive interruption in spirit, mind, and body, yet we have seen the more obvious damaging effects across cultures in the historical prevalence of sexual unfaithfulness and sexual violations that most often leave the ones affected desolate (2 Samuel 13). I will share this excerpt with you from a human analysis I delivered a few years ago at the Breaking the Silence Conference in Ottawa: "For, in fact, the act of rape is not driven only by cultural, societal, or global silence but by an ultimate reality of disconnection and inner-psychological silencing of both men and women."

Okay, let's breathe. How O.M.G. is it to see that such a reality of maladaptive interruption in history is still so evidently entrenched in the collective reality today? Unfaithfulness on every level is an abnormal norm that has deeply affected the reality that God intended for us to live through faithful love in relationship, marriage, and family.

"Let us discern for ourselves what is right; let us learn together what is good" (Job 34:4 NIV). Commit to never again trumpet the legacy of slavery or any maladaptive reality above the "in the beginning" and redeemed legacy of good things in God through Christ.

God's Intention	Maladaptive Interruption
In the Beginning Faithful Pattern of Relationship A unified, faithful family system	**Slavery** The radical separation of relationship and families, broken family system, mental slavery belief system
Unblocked God-human communion	Personal God-human relationship sometimes blocked through institutional violation
Affirmation for him; Security for her	Violated, insecure historical woman Emasculated historical man, loss of needed respect, affirmation, and power
Marriage celebrated and prepared for	Outlawed marriage, outlawed sacred space Outlawed faithful private & public emtional connection
Intimacy honoured as sacred	Abased physical focus Hidden sexuality & destructive violation through sexuality
Generational legacy of bold love	Broken family system Enslaved belief system
Families together create a protective & safe community	Generational disconnetion & diminished sense of community

Interrupt the Interruption

Without minimizing the intensity of any internal pain, can I invite you to suspend blame, fault, judgment, or shame even for a moment? I know that this may be difficult to do, but let's look behind the scenes. When we intently look at the maladaptive interruptions in relationship, from the past to today, is it that the historical woman has lived a reality of such deep violation and insecurity for so long that she has become closed to her true identity and to him? As one who has an innate drive to nurture and feel, has she functionally become independent in an actual fight for the safety of her own heart, ever so often saying, "I don't need him," yet, in fact, really resisting the pain and brokenness of heart that he—the historical man—represents? At the same time, is it that the historical man has battled in the past, both spiritually and naturally, with his heart but repeatedly, without apt reward, has found it hard to bounce back and so has become shut down or disconnected? Is it that, as a result, he now unwittingly relates from his innate physical ability, instead? Has he been emasculated over time by a historical reality that robbed him of the freedom and affirmation he needed to hold on to his heart's capacity and God-given identity? Is he yet struggling to restore the capacity of his heart that has been shut down? Are both the historical man and woman still unconsciously entrapped in a system of unfaithfulness and legacy of slavery that is void of their true identity? Corrective interruption is crucial. Let us truly do a heart check-up to rediscover, revive, reignite, and restore the heart of who we are.

Pause with me for a moment and flex your internal muscles. Say this with me, "I will be bold. I will value the truth of who I am in God. I believe that I was created free to love. I am committed to walking out this freedom in my decisions. I refuse to consciously or unconsciously participate in the bondage of my past." Now, according to the declaration of God for relationships in this season, I declare with you that you will recover all.

"So David inquired of the LORD, saying, 'Shall I pursue this troop? Shall I overtake them?' And He answered him, 'Pursue, for you shall surely overtake them and without fail recover all.'" (1 Samuel 30:8)

"Let's be clear, the Anointed One has set us free – not partially, but completely and wonderfully free! We must always cherish this truth and stubbornly refuse to go back into the bondage of our past." (Galatians 5:1 TPT)

Boldly turn away from a maladaptive interruption paradigm in every relationship. Interrupt the interruption.

Ongoing Practical Application

Look beyond your relationship as it is today, and truly see from the past who has separated you from the love that God intended. Rediscover the spirit of maladaptive interruptions and the misguided belief system that serves to maintain entrapment. You will realize that who you are deep within is much greater than the negatives of history and any maladaptive experience you have been confronted with. You will then see this scripture from a fresh perspective:

"Who shall separate us from the love of Christ? Shall tribulation, or distress, or persecution, or famine, or nakedness, or peril, or sword? As it is written: 'For Your sake we are killed all day long; we are accounted as sheep for the slaughter.' Yet in all these things we are more than conquerors through Him who loved us. For I am persuaded that neither death nor life, nor angels nor principalities nor powers, nor things present nor things to come, nor height nor depth, nor any other created thing, shall be able to separate us from the love of God which is in Christ Jesus our Lord" (Romans 8:35–39).

Without minimizing the intensity of your past experiences, take on a more-than-a-conqueror mindset and become increasingly aware that who you've needed to wrestle with is not so much the represented historical man or woman in your life but rather the actual spirit of that maladaptive interruption thing. One client said it so well in her own rediscovery process beyond a history of relationship injury with her mother. She said, "She didn't know that she didn't know." This awareness of a lack of awareness in the ones we not only hold accountable for our pain but have also long looked to for our healing can be one of the most liberating realizations towards new beginnings. If the life force or belief system of maladaptive interruptions is eliminated, then the negative effects can no longer be perpetuated.

The truth is, we have

Correctively interrupt every destructive pattern resulting from maladaptive interruptions.

all consciously or unconsciously participated in some maladaptive things without sometimes knowing the true impact of what we did (Romans 3:23). Just ask my principal from way back then if he knew that I would still remember the negative impact of those straps now at forty-something, and he will most likely say, "No, only discipline was my intention." Your reality could be way more intense than this. It is, however, important not to minimize on both sides. We are all a work in progress. Correctively interrupt every destructive pattern resulting from maladaptive interruptions.

You may further relate to a common picture of young siblings in trouble, trying hard to gain favour with a parent by pointing fingers at each other as they explain who was really at fault for spilling the drink. The parent then instinctively responds, "It doesn't matter whose fault it is. Both of you go clean up the mess." Well, I'm not saying that it really doesn't matter whose fault it is when it comes to maladaptive interruptions. What I do know is that there is great wisdom in this parent's obvious desire to get things back to the way they were before the mess. When we set aside who is to blame or who is at fault, even for a moment, it truly unblocks the heart and makes room for a more empowered stance to move forward. What we let go of God takes care of, as it allows us to invite Him into our hearts. Yet He is a good Father to all of us.

The elders back then would say with great passion: "Don't hold people in your heart." So, for a moment, see the damage from a history of maladaptive interruptions in both your heart and the other person's heart. Then by taking the driver's seat, you will be able to move yourself forward, and one step at a time free your heart to bring progressive and sustainable healing. I know it is counter intuitive and not automatic. It has to be intentional. It works.

In Your Immediate Relationship

Refuse to be entrapped by the words of your lips (Proverbs 6:2). Make every effort to see more of God and more possibilities for new beginnings in your heart and relationship. Focusing away from blame and more on the God-factor is like turning on the light that confounds the darkness and proverbial monsters. It will make a difference. Seize every opportunity to build up rather than destroy him or her. Strategically destroy the maladaptive interruption and destructive pattern. By doing this you will make room and increase the destined opportunity to restore *the heart of a good thing.*

Let's do this. It is possible.

Step 1

A Heart Check-Up

An invitation to safe willingness of heart.
Be willing to do the work that your heart and
the heart of your relationship needs.

*"Trust in the LORD WITH ALL YOUR HEART,
and lean not on your own understanding;
in all your ways acknowledge Him, and He
shall direct your paths."* (Proverbs 3:5-6)

A Heart Check-Up

Recently, I received several letters in the mail inviting me to initiate a particular medical screening. I must admit, it chimed my internal bell of vulnerability and gave rise to many "what if" questions. What if I open myself to this and the outcome is negative? What if I find out what I don't want to know? What if...what if...what if...? There was very little processed about the potential positives that could also be attached to this initiative. I simply filed the letter away and went on with business as usual. The truth is, it is human to ignore even important things, especially when such things chime a bell of vulnerability in us.

A willing heart is the key that opens the door for new beginnings. Informed readiness of heart to engage with God's initiative for our lives, in every stage of life, is crucial. No matter how difficult the decision, it is one of the most important steps that you must take before the process of ultimate restoration and new beginnings can begin. This first starts with you and then becomes a function in your relationship. The key is willingness; willingness to do the work that your heart and the heart of your relationship needs. A willing heart is aware and remains open enough to hear the truth. It is open enough not just to the loudest "what if" voice, but also to the truth in the safest voice.

"The Lord is near to those who have a broken heart, and saves such as have a contrite spirit." (Psalm 34:18)

"Truth's shining light guides me in my choices and decisions; the revelation of your word makes my pathway clear." (Psalm 119:105 TPT)

God is inviting you to experience healing and enrichment in all dimensions of relationship. This is an invitation to an intentional choice, beyond business as usual. A willingness of heart will fuel your ability to do what is helpful, not just what you've always done. *"If you are willing and obedient, you will eat the good things of the land"* (Isaiah 1:19 NIV). Are you willing?

Your heart is the focus of God's attention. You are the apple of His eye. Willingness from this place of vulnerability is a godly sacrifice. David really understood this when he experienced one of the worst relationship blunders of his life. He realized then that beyond any other sacrifice, willingness and vulnerability of heart are what God requires in order to restore good things, even when it seems impossible. It first starts with opening your heart, one step at a time. *"For You do not desire sacrifice, or else I would give it; You do not delight in burnt offering. The sacrifices of God are a broken spirit, a broken and a contrite heart, these, O God, You will not despise"*(Psalm 51:16–17).

Being willing does not mean that any negative experiences are minimized, neither does it shun the intensity of any pain. The journey of willingness may not come naturally. What it means is that you desire to experience healing or new beginnings, and you intentionally choose to open your heart with this as your focus. When you are faced with conflict in a good relationship, it is even more important that you intentionally keep your heart open to engage. Purposely refocus beyond the automatic response of business as usual. Acknowledge that who you are in Christ, what your heart really needs, and the legacy of bold love that you are created to live as a witness are more important than the unfinished thing or the person you may be filing away. Be willing to make tough decisions, to work on what you should, to end only what's not God ordained, and to grow through difficultly and pain.

Being open to a heart check-up will lead you to a place where you are able to slow down long enough to hear the truth in silence, and even in a noisy world. It is a process that requires you to be present to the genuine reality of your heart, with a focus on the promised blessing of God.

"A new heart also will I give you, and a new spirit will I put within you: and I will take away the stony heart out of your flesh, and I will give you an heart of flesh. And I will put my spirit within you, and cause you to walk in my statutes, and ye shall keep my judgments, and do them. And ye shall dwell in the land that I gave to your fathers; and ye shall be my people, and I will be your God."(Ezekiel 36:26-28 KJV)

Are you willing?

Matters of the Heart
Risking where it is safe keeps the heart alive

♥

Have you ever seen a knockout in a boxing match? When the brain is hit with such force, it actually shuts down, at least for a bit, in response to the trauma and in order to survive. Our emotional heart also shuts down at times to survive when we are hit hard by life, just like the alive yet seemingly lifeless man or woman we see in the ring after that knockout. In that moment, shutting down is logical and safe, instead of willingly staying open. However, without the right awareness and effective next steps, what was meant to be a moment of safety or self-protection can actually lure you into staying in this mode far beyond what is helpful.

When the heart is broken or shuts down, and remains this way for an extended period of time, a reality of heartlessness becomes the norm, and willingness is also shut down. Heartlessness hurts self and others consciously and unconsciously, because a heart that is meant to love is closed. What may start as a natural, protective response becomes a progressively non-feeling heart that really needs to feel, even when it sometimes hurt, in order to effectively love and be loved. Counter to what we truly desire deep inside, coping through an unwilling shut-down heart creates a legacy of dysfunctional realities, and is both a reinforcement and outcome of the maladaptive paradigm in relationship.

Willingness: A Story of Blame, Self Identity, & Empowered Responsibility

A young woman has struggled significantly to make safe choices in relationship. She has just experienced what she describes as a "huge betrayal." She says, "My heart hurts. My heart is broken." She then explains that she has made a decision not to trust anyone, not even those who may be safe enough. From a place of deeper meaning, she has made a decision to shut down her heart, at least in part, because this feels safer than being hurt.

Tracking back a little, this young woman rediscovers how her heart has, in fact, been affected throughout her upbringing, as she has experienced a history of neglect and abandonment connected to a negative father-daughter relationship. She explained that while he worked hard to provide financially, his heart was emotionally unavailable or shut down. She recalls longing for a heart connection

Our emotional heart shuts down at times to survive when we are hit hard by life.

with him, but acknowledges that this has remained outstanding. In her world, she blames him as the one who should have taught her how to keep her heart alive and faithful, especially after her relationship knockouts. She also blames him for her limited relationship capacity now. What she has come to believe is that relationships that should be safe actually hurt. This experience hurts, even now.

Let's change this story to include any other male, female, leader, or caregiver, then this may reflect some part of all our lives. The reality is, when the heart is repeatedly broken or knocked out it shuts down, and the essential senses that support the entire body's functioning also shut down. Like the young lady, this affects our ability to make effective relationship decisions. Far beyond the natural, because the entire body is dependent on the health of the heart, when the heart shuts down the essential senses in the entire body also progressively shut down. The health of the heart affects our willingness to engage with new beginnings, and this really does affect our entire life in relationship. When an individual is consciously or unconsciously shut down, relationship connection is also led with limited sense.

The Reality of Our Five Senses When the Heart Shuts Down

A Heartless Relationship Is a Headless Relationship

We have five traditionally recognized senses, all of which are located in the head, expect one — touch.

When the heart shuts down:

- Vision and effective foresight for your relationship goes progressively blind. The sense of sight is significantly interrupted *"If people can't see what God is doing, they stumble all over themselves; but when they attend to what he reveals, they are most blessed"* (Proverbs 29:18 MSG).

- Hearing God's instruction for your heart and relationship goes progressively deaf. Your sense of hearing, or faith that comes by hearing, is significantly interrupted *"So then faith comes* by hearing, and hearing by the word of God" (Romans 10:17).

❤ The ability to speak well of your heart condition, relationship, or the other person goes progressively mute. Your sense of taste, or testimony that defeats the enemy, is significantly interrupted *"Oh, taste and see that the* LORD *is good; blessed is the man who trusts in Him!"*(Psalm 43:8). *"And they overcame him by the blood of the Lamb and by the word of their testimony"* (Revelation 12:11).

❤ Discernment beyond the obvious is progressively diminished. Unconscious business as usual remains the norm. Your sense of smell, or discernment, is significantly interrupted*"Who is wise? Let him understand these things. Who is prudent? Let him know them. For the ways of the* LORD *are right; the righteous walk in them, but transgressors stumble in them"* (Hosea 14:9).

When heartlessness prevails, we inadvertently allow the only sense that is outside of the head to also reign. A heartless relationship then defaults to becoming physically driven and misguided, with limited access to needed senses. Like the first historical man and woman after the fall, brokenness of heart today, without a heart check-up, perpetuates a mostly physical reality driven by the sense of touch as the default towards meeting an otherwise genuine need for relationship. Guided by a lack of vision, faith, a good-thing testimony, and discernment, such a relationship is more likely to be deeply damaging, consciously and unconsciously. Sensible awareness and willingness are required to restore the heart's needed capacity. How is your heart?

Beyond Past & Present Knockouts

When this young woman was asked, "Would your father say that his desire was to hurt or damage your heart?" with a sense of judgment in her eyes, she replied, "He would say no. He doesn't think he's done anything wrong."

She was then asked, "But is your heart hurt? Is your heart damaged?"

She said, assuredly, "Yes."

Grappling to make sense of her experience now, without minimizing her pain, she realizes that it is vitally important for her to chart an intentional pathway away from being the kind of shut-down heart that she's come to know causes hurt and damage. She recognizes that the kind of heart she herself has been avoiding from the outside now looks like the one on the inside. This wasn't a conscious decision. She now saw the option to begin living the kind of heart and connection she's truly longed for — a heart that remains open, even through the hurts, with a focus on moving forward. For her, this doesn't feel comfortable, because it is not familiar, but she is willing to do the work, and acknowledges that it is time to revive what she needs from a place of empowered responsibility within. She owns what is in her control towards restoring a heart that is able to risk where it is safe, and securely love and be loved. She puts it this way, "The best thing I can do is keep my heart alive."

This young lady sees that blaming and maintaining this as the focus, while seemingly justified, has until now blocked her from the possibility of needed new beginnings. She now owns the power within to correctively interrupt the draining sting of blaming the ones who have failed her heart, by reaching to restore her heart from inside. She is also now able to see into her father's potential reality—the other story. From her progressively unblocked heart, she sees her father's own interrupted reality. She sees his potential struggle with a heartless journey of his own, which has unwittingly limited his heart's capacity. Maybe he "doesn't know that he doesn't know" how much the damage has been intense and real. Maybe, reflecting on the historical man continuum, he has inadvertently lived a default and robust physical life, coping maladaptively with too many knockouts in his own history.

With close attention to what was and how it now affects what is, maybe the story above is a key example of how an unconscious legacy of maladaptive interruption is reinforced from generation to generation, if not correctively interrupted. When you are willing and stay open to matters of the heart, you will be touched by all of your senses to restore an active heart through the paradigm of bold love. That is a good thing.

Be encouraged by the model of what God did for you, and commit to being willing to do the same. *"But God demonstrates His own love toward us, in that while we were still sinners, Christ died for us. For if we were enemies we were reconciled to God through the death of His Son, much more, having been reconciled, we shall be saved by His life"* (Romans 5:8 &10). Your heart is a priority to God. Your heart is the key to love—"the greatest of these." So even if your spiritual life is intense and your physical life is robust, without a willing and attuned, functioning heart, the greatest of these will remain silent or hidden. Your success in love hinges on the willingness and wellness of your heart (3 John 1:2). Love is your life-giving source, and a willing heart is your instrument. That is why Jesus, through the new garden, became a guarantor, as the mediator between God and us (1 Timothy 2:5). In this, He became the ultimate heart source and pathway for love to descend as His willing gift to us, instead of choosing what was justified blame. This demonstrated willingness, with a clear restoration goal, is precise. So, like Christ, when we do our best to release the wrongs of others and willingly focus on restoring a God pattern of love in our heart instead, we will restore needed life in what would have otherwise remained heartless, senseless, damaging, or dead. *"But God still loved us with such great love. He is so rich in compassion and mercy. Even when we were dead and doomed in our many sins, he united us into the very life of Christ and saved us by his wonderful grace! He raised us up with Christ the exalted One, and we ascended with him into the glorious perfection and authority of the heavenly realm, for we are now co-seated as one with Christ!"* (Ephesians 2:4-6 TPT).

Are you willing?

Moving Forward

Say with me, "I am willing. I am willing to love. I am willing to live the model of God's great love in relationship with myself, with others, and in marriage. God, I ask that you increase my capacity to hear the writing of your love in my heart, in Jesus' name. Amen."

Prayer

An important first step towards willingness of heart is prayer. Know that communicating with God will effectively support you to take the steps you are called to take, especially when willingness challenges your view of the situation you face. Use the strength of Scripture to remind yourself of God's safe presence in you, and affirm your willingness to do what's effective, wherever you are in your life and relationship.

Brain Power
Get Going Again

Our brain is like a storage file. It only identifies effectively with information that is already familiar in storage. So when you introduce something new, even something amazing, because it is unfamiliar with the existing storage, it is often eventually discarded. So repeating, again and again, "I am willing" as a new reality helps to build a new option for your brain that is then called to bear when it is most needed. Repeating every new step, again and again, will make it familiar and thus gives it a secure claim to referencing space in your brain's filing. This is a sure way to unlearn the past and maintain new beginnings. *Prayer Therapy for Brain-Mind-Heart Renewal* by my good friend Rev. Marva Tyndale will support you with helpful insights regarding specific prayer for the brain.

So whenever you are prompted, whether by an experience of joy or pain, own the safety of God's promise, and whisper, again and again, to your brain, "I am willing. I am willing to love." Try it the next time you are in the midst of a fight with your significant other and see the difference in your brain's choice of options as a response. Know that even in such a place of vulnerability, your heart and brain will become increasingly receptive to the new. One step at a time, you will gain more and more capacity to activate bold love in your relationship.

A willing heart in the right relationship will change your life in unimaginable ways. As a dear friend said, "For many of us, willingness is an achievement in itself." So be proud of yourself for taking this brave step. Now think about that relationship in question, and begin to practice, at least with your brain. Whether it is to move beyond any negative experience or conflict, or to increase the volume of boldness in your loving, are you willing? Go ahead and bring that person to mind, including yourself, and echo with your brain, "I am willing. I am willing to love."

Ongoing Practical Application

- ♥ Pay attention to patterns in your relationship interactions. Blame, which includes fault or judgment, is one of the first signs that you are participating in and reinforcing the maladaptive interruption paradigm. If you think about it on a fairness scale, what may have been done to you may not compare to what you have done. Yet when it comes to ordained relationships, letting go makes room in your heart and is a sure way of moving forward. *"Judge not, that you be not judged"* (Matthew 7:1)

- Without minimizing your pain, see the hidden agenda. See the "other story," and own the empowered responsibility to move forward and maintain your God-given identity

- Reflect on the original version of love, which means to give. Remember how Christ sacrificed for you. Then challenge yourself to give through the corrective paradigm of bold love

- Risk where you are safe enough—this will keep your heart alive. If you fail to risk in love, you also risk not becoming free to experience love.

Step 2

ReDiscover

ReDiscover who you are—your identity, purpose, and role, as God intended, apart from every maladaptive interruption.

"Who knows the thoughts that another person has? Only a person's spirit that lives within him knows his thoughts. It is the same with God. No one knows the thoughts of God except the Spirit of God" (1 Corinthians2:11).

Re*Discover*
Who are You?

⸺ ♥ ⸺

Every great revelation begins with a great question (Matthew 16:13–19). Can you imagine who you would be if who you were created to be was never interrupted? Can you imagine beyond history, culture, family of origin issues, brokenness, or trauma who God created you to be deep within? Can you imagine who you would be, across relationships, if your heart was completely free to love and be loved at full-potential capacity? Pause for a moment and consider. In spite of, or even because of, every past thing, the truth about who you are is most importantly reflected through the Word of God. You are a blessing. You are a great gift. You are the heart of a good thing.

Who you are as an individual determines who you are in relationship. Most of us have struggled at one point or another to understand who we are. We define ourselves or are defined by others. We compare ourselves to others, then doubt who we are, and sometimes we become another self altogether to meet a need for belonging. Who you are includes your personality, goals, needs, purpose, strengths, and stuff. It is your authentic self, one that is often informed by the various relationship systems that have impacted your life. Understanding your identity is a key factor in the choices you make in relationship.

To rediscover is to become fully aware, again, of who you are in spite of, or even because of, where you have been. It is an intentional process of becoming increasingly conscious of your strengths – God's wealth within – and your stuff – everything that has interrupted this. It is also seeking to understand your purpose in life and in every relationship. Having a mindset that is biased towards your best success really helps. *"Call to Me, and I will answer you, and show you great and mighty things, which you do not know"* (Jeremiah 33:3).

To rediscover is to first seek to know God's definition and purpose for the authentic you. Do you know who you really are? *"But you are a chosen generation, a royal priesthood, a holy nation, His own special people, that you may proclaim the praises of Him who called you out of darkness into His marvelous light"* (1 Peter 2:9). To rediscover is to also symbolically, and literally, look at yourself in a mirror and remain there long enough to see who you see, beyond what your eyes can see. It is ongoing willingness and vulnerability to both acknowledge your strengths and to also confront and unlearn the negative interruptions It is ongoing willingness and vulnerability to both acknowledge your strengths and to also confront and unlearn the negative interruptions of your past. To rediscover is to

Who you are as an individual determines who you are in relationship.

consciously acknowledge what you know. It is seeing the reality of how both your strengths and stuff have contributed to the way you do relationship with self, others, or your spouse. It is then engaging with a responsible goal to maintain awareness and remain open to becoming who you are designed to be at full potential.

The process of rediscovering who you truly are is an ongoing one. When you know who you are, your identity will become like a protective stance. Then the intrusion of maladaptive interruptions will become less likely.

Who are you?

Ongoing Practical Application C.A.R.E. to Re*Discover* Who You Are:

C – Communicate by giving voice to what's in your heart. Give an audible voice to what may have been silenced inside. Who are you? What are the goals in your heart? What is your purpose? What is your personality style? If you don't know this, do a Gary Smalley personality questionnaire online. It is enlightening.

Start this *communicate* process in safety with yourself, and reach out for support as needed. Go beyond just here and now to unearth the influence of culture, family of origin, and the past. If you are in a safe enough relationship, communicate your awareness, goals, purpose, and personality with that individual. Opportunities to share in a safe relationship will magnify the benefits of awareness, growth, or needed healing. Don't be silent or silenced. Rediscover what's in your heart and who you are.

A – Acknowledge your strengths and address your stuff. All of us have some strengths and some stuff. It is counterproductive when things work silently, especially if they work to destroy us, or even when they work well, and we are unaware of their presence. Ask God to help you remember what is important to remember. Then address what comes to awareness. Seek ongoing understanding of your desires, goal, purpose, and who you are designed to be in relationship (Proverbs 4:7).

R – Redefine who you are by whose you are, whenever you get stuck. Who you were created to be should be your first reference. Be open to learning something new to support new beginnings in your relationship with self, others, and your spouse from this first reference. It takes discipline to truly slow down long enough to rediscover yourself, even when it's about good things. So be disciplined, own the benefit, and do it continually. Make room for uninterrupted access to your authentic identity. You are worth the gift of knowing who you are.

E - Encourage yourself often (1 Samuel 30:6). You are a great gift to the relationships that God has placed in your life. We are all growing into the fullness of who God created us to be, and there are strengths in everyone. Build a bank of good things by appreciating yourself. This currency will help you to maintain an increasing balance of strengths to confront the tough stuff on an ongoing basis.

A Picture of You
I Am a Man of Honour

I Am a Man of Honour

At my core, I am a man of great wisdom

A visionary, an ordained planter of seed

One destined to be a priest, even far beyond what eyes can see

I am a hero, warrior, leader, lion, and yet a lamb

I am a man of honour

I have an uncommon depth of wealth within

My potential for generational influence is yet so deep

I am a destined forerunner in my unique lane

I am designed to leap beyond every mountain

I have the blessing of new beginnings; there is grace for every day to come

The surpassing greatness of God's power is towards me

As a brother, uncle, nephew, father, husband, friend, and son

I am a hero, warrior, leader, lion, yet a lamb

I am a man of honour and the heart of a good thing

When Purpose Meets Your Role

It is an amazing thing to practically apply scriptural revelation to everyday life. Like the mighty men of 1 Chronicles 12, including the sons of Issachar who understood the times and knew what Israel ought to do (vs. 32), every man has an incredible gift within his heart to understand the time and access divine seed. He is also called to secure the environment and quality of this seed, which then determines the quality of reaping through the woman who is designed to nurture, carry, and multiply such a seed to life. When men plant seeds in relationship with faithfulness and love, incredible doors of possibilities for good things are opened in the harvest to come.

God has given every man seed — a vision, a purpose, and a calling. Whether realized or yet to be rediscovered, every man has this seed. It is a dimensional seed that cannot come to life without a suitable helper: the woman who is a wife. This is the wisdom of Genesis 2:18, which goes far beyond a physical reference. *"It is not good for man to be alone"* reflects that the good thing is for the two to be joined together as one, on dimensional levels, in order to bear an intended relationship harvest.

Sowing with an "In the Beginning" Identity

I remember growing up in a time when farming was a key source of income in the community. The process of sowing and reaping was always fascinating to me. I particularly remember my uncle, who was a farmer, and how he engaged with farming meticulously. Uncle was a devout follower of Jesus, who valued attending church regularly. Yet even on a usual church day, he would either leave early or not attend church at all when he understood that it was time to fulfill his role through planting. After my curious questions, he explained that he understood it was the precise time to plant because the moon — symbolic environment — was in the right position. In this right position, the moon pulls to the surface of the soil what truly matters — water-symbolic Word — from deep within the earth. This right position of the moon, indicating the right level of water in the soil, ultimately encouraged the best growth from whatever seed was planted. The fascinating thing is that my uncle was more often successful than not in his harvest. It was no doubt correlated to his keen understanding of who he is and his role. He continued to prioritize this level of awareness needed to secure the best environment — relationship — when and where his seed would be planted. It was the key principles towards the best outcome. This is a good picture of a rediscovered man, one who is prepared to be *the heart of a good thing* husband.

Can you imagine the increasingly good fruit you would reap, continually, if you understood who you truly are and, as a result, only plant seed by first ensuring that the Word is in the right position in your relationship with self, others, and your spouse? Uncle's awareness and focus on understanding the environment moved him to intentionally act according to this understanding, which also meant that everything else became secondary, even valued church attendance.

Being informed enough of who you are will allow you to sow the right seed at the right time, with the right level of water — Word — in the soil of your relationship. This is your prescribed number one priority. The strongest prevailing principle or environment in every great relationship is your identity and the Word of God. This is the art of seedtime that guarantees an intended harvest.

I Am Woman

I am worthy of esteem

I am a great gift

A destined generational lifeline for so many

Even when challenged at my core

I am a heart of strength, vulnerability, and profound capacity

I am beautiful in so many ways

I am unique in great depth, resilience, and character

In all I face, I am the beloved of God

I am crowned with grace and honour by my heavenly Father

A true nurturer of souls, a creative life force

A heart of strength, vulnerability, yet profound capacity

I am the heart of a good thing

I am woman.

I remember growing up and being fascinated with how the women in my family seemed so biblical. They just had a way of creating something out of next to nothing. Like many women today, they had an amazing ability to somehow multiply a seed. One moment, it seemed as though there were very little ingredients in the kitchen, yet the next moment there would be a full-blown meal that ended up feeding more than expected, all from seemingly nothing in the first place. This was the art of multiplying the good things and making them so much more than they would have otherwise been. Women just have this thing; it's a quality, a unique ability. *"She is like the merchant ships, she brings her food from afar. Strength and honour are her clothing; she shall rejoice in time to come"* (Proverbs 31:14; 25 NKJV).

Women truly have this unshakeable ability to catch what seems like just a seed, hold on to it, nurture it, multiply it, and bring it to life, multiplied. This is why the type of seed planted is so important. For, while multiplying works with the good things, it also works with the stuff of life. If the seed is good, women multiply it. If it is not so good, it is also multiplied. Knowing who you are as a woman will allow you to intentionally choose what you carry, or not, so that what you multiply will be intentional.

A rediscovered woman, who knows her true identity, is prepared to be a wife.

A rediscovered woman who knows her true identity is prepared to be a wife. She brings a vital life force to a rediscovered man. What would have otherwise remained just a seed is now multiplied and brought to life. The wealth of promised favour to a rediscovered man, *"he who finds a wife,"* is now manifested through her. She is a favour channel. Here, beyond the seed, an intended biblical legacy becomes reality through this relationship, in favour from the Lord (Proverbs 18:22).

Comparable Identity through Roles

So as men and women in relationship, we are equally vital. While by design we are different, we are yet comparable. One without the other is incomplete. Ultimately, when such a synergy is lived in the marital relationship, an incredible no-eye-has-seen-no-ear-has-heard, bold love becomes an ongoing reality and a privileged gift. Only when a relationship isn't really blissful does the focus of conversation become who is the boss of whom. The real goal in successful relationships is to understand, respect, and complement comparable roles. The process of preparation before coming together is as important as the process after.

So who should take the initiative when it comes to the need for restoration and new beginnings in a relationship? The answer is: whoever does. Whoever discerns the need for restoration initiates the process, with wisdom as the principle thing and with understanding (Proverbs 4:7).

Commit to rediscovering the depth of who you are, and bringing such a depth to your relationship, and open possibilities beyond the seed for favour. Favour in awareness, favour in identity, favour in love, and favour in tangible things. Now let's use the strength of who you are to revive some good things that were otherwise disappearing yet needed.

Step 3

ReVive

ReVive your heartbeat to discern and investigate interruptions and blockages.

Take intentional steps to regain what your heart, and the heart of your relationship, needs to live — love.

ReVive what was disappearing, but intended, and cause *the heart of a good thing* to come to life, again.

"And the peace of God, which surpasses all understanding, will guard your hearts and minds through Christ Jesus" (Philippians 4:7).

Re*Vive*
What Your Heart
Needs Is Love

A heart attack is a seriously detrimental thing, which is typically caused in the natural by the lack of oxygen-rich blood to the heart due to a buildup of blockages. It is not uncommon for such blockages to go unnoticed by the one whose heart is being affected. Natural things often reflect the principle of spiritual and mental things. When this symbolic instrument of love is attacked by the accumulation of what has been, literally nothing else matters more than to revive life to the heart, because the entire body depends on it to live. This is also true when it comes to bringing the heart of a good thing back to life.

"So above all, guard the affections of your heart, for they affect all that you are. Pay attention to the welfare of your innermost being, for from there flows the wellspring of life"
(Proverbs 4:23 TPT).

A Bypass Intervention

You may relate to someone who has had a bypass surgery. Typically, what happens in this process is both an acknowledgement of the blockage and the use of other healthy arteries in the body to bypass what was interrupted thus bringing back what the heart needs by unblocking the flow. Just as the natural heart needs oxygen-rich blood, so does the emotional heart need love. Reviving your own heart, or the heart of your relationship, mirrors the bypass process. It means that you intentionally discern, investigate, and then work from existing strengths to bypass the blockages. Your heart will then regain the love channel it needs to boldly love and live. This is a process that is vital for everyone, especially everyone who is in a God-ordained relationship and realizes the need to bring back pathways to full potential by unblocking the flow of the good things that were otherwise silently disappearing. This process will awaken an affirming truth within: you can love fully, again, even after your heart has been attacked or interrupted.

The process of reviving will support you in uncovering and removing the conscious and unconscious things that have been a blockage in your capacity to love boldly. It means freeing your heart from any build-up of the maladaptive interruption by taking necessary steps to restore a corrective flow of bold love. A genuine reviving process must be powered by faith-filled confidence that godly revelation will ultimately be the source of new beginnings, upon this rock. *"And I will give you the keys of the kingdom of heaven, and whatever you bind on earth will be bound in heaven, and whatever you loose on earth will be loosed in heaven"* (Matthew 16:19).

Pay Attention to the Child Within

"He heals the brokenhearted and binds up their wounds"
(Psalm 147:3)

In every woman there is yet a little girl, and, likewise, a little boy in every man. This little child in all of us seeks love and healing all the more, especially when this need was foundationally blocked or unmet. Each day I sit together with adult individuals in the safety of a counselling room, and as I also reflect on my own story, I am keenly reminded that the heart of this little girl or little boy has a very important story to tell, but one that is often silent or silenced. Taking the time to really listen to this story from this child within can make you wise in insight and reveal a crucial pathway to revive anything that has been blocked or missing.

If you only attend to the adult man or woman that everyone sees but fail to gain genuine awareness of the child within, you unwittingly add to him or her being silenced. If he or she is silenced, we often see surface evidence of an internal tension through seemingly childlike relationship tantrums and mental health. These are all symptoms, not so much of commonly assumed intentional bad behaviour, but of the underlying blockage or unresolved reality itself.

A Demonstrated Reality

A young man shared his story about growing up without a present father. He noted that he really hadn't shared this story before because he believed "no one would get how messed up it was." He explained how his father was involved in multiple relationships and had several children with different women. Growing up with his mother and siblings got really "rough." He started to act out. He was then separated from his family and grew up in an institution. This young man remembers being perceived as a "rude handful" growing up and, as a result, was shunned. He began to believe then that he wasn't worthy enough to be accepted by his family, just because.

Now fast forward with this young man to his adult reality. He now has several children of his own with several different women. He acknowledges that, "My weakness is when a woman tells me I look good." He then becomes sexually involved. Making sense of his lifelong reality, he sees an unmet need for acceptance, belonging, self worth, and affirmation in his heart. The child within has had a longing that was blocked and remained stored, unresolved. He further sees something that seems nothing short of a mystery. He says, "Oh my God, my dad wasn't even there for me, not even a remnant of him was present, but today I am so much like him." An otherwise accomplished man can yet long for the childhood affirmation of his father and act out this void through relationships. His bypass from repeating this negative pattern is to discern the need, and from awareness of his God-given identity, genuinely love and affirm himself. It pays to pay attention to the child. For while you are holding the adult accountable, it may really be the unhealed child within him or her that's misbehaving.

Similarly, a female shared her story of having experienced the trauma of sexual violation as a child. She felt tainted and unlovable as a result. She explained having held this experience inside in silence, as she believed her voice would not be heard or accepted as true. It's been like "a demon inside." The heart blockage is real. For many years, the darkness of this experience has expressed itself through symptoms of depression, self hatred, and anxiety.

Through good supports, this young woman has come to realize that it is important for her to revive her heart beyond this overwhelming blockage. Her bypass is to give this child within an empowered voice and to also be the best friend who now listens to the important truth this little girl has to share. By doing this, she progressively diminishes the blockage of a negative identity that was shaped through trauma, darkness, and silence. She now charts a pathway to revive her heart through the strength of who she really is, as created by God.

The truth is, our present reality in relationship and marriage is deeply informed or blocked by our childhood experiences, which are often inadequately resolved and stored in conscious and unconscious memory. Whenever situations in the present resemble this past experience, we are likely to react as though now is really then, in how we engage, disengage, or freeze in our emotions. Since most childhood injures happen in the context of relationship, relationship is then a most common trigger in resemblance for many.

Whether your primary story is one connected to family of origin, culture, spiritual or personal experiences, we all have a childhood story that we need to be familiar with. It is important to discern and investigate how this story contributes to either balance or tilt the scale on which you weigh relationships. Every effort should be made to become familiar with the heart of the child within as you seek to create a clear flow to love beyond what was interrupted or missing. Ignoring his or her reality is not effective, because being blocked from who you are inside often also means being relationally blocked as well.

As a psychotherapist, I am aware that individuals who struggle with particular mental illnesses hear voices within. This is certainly not that. Paying attention to the child within is the action you take to truly listen to the silent or silenced voice of who you are within. Even though it may seem weird, check in with that child. Listen keenly to the strengths and the stuff. Listen to the story that you need to hear beyond your outer ears.

Engaging with this process will open a unique opportunity to bring to life again a renewed sense of meaning to a story that may have been silent, silenced, or disappearing. With the right support, this can be an incredibly awakening process, as you intentionally gain insight and become unblocked. Be courageous and willing enough to listen. You will no doubt hear the voice of a deeply meaningful story, one that you need to hear from a heart that needs bold love. Know that the child within is dependent on you, the adult, to unblock the way needed to revive the full potential to your heart from within.

Ongoing Practical Application

- ❤ Check in with the child within

- ❤ Reach out for appropriate support as needed

- ❤ Pay attention and listen to this important story that needs to be heard

- ❤ Give a voice to that story from an empowerment narrative

- ❤ Revive effective meaning and bypass the blockage from knowing who you are as God intended

- ❤ Your heart needs to align in health with the child inside

Focus on the Need
Beyond the Conflict

ohnny, Lisa's husband, was on his way home from work and was caught in really bad traffic. He then also realized that his phone battery was dead. He is a creature-of-habit kind of guy, and would normally be home by 6:30 p.m. However, it was now about 8:00 p.m., and he had no way of communicating with his wife about his delay. Meanwhile, Lisa was calling him back to back, with no answer. She'd become progressively concerned, then upset, and then scared by thoughts of something having gone very wrong. It was about 9:00 p.m. when Johnny finally walked through the door. Lisa immediately approached him and, with an angry voice, yelled, "Where have you been?" He yelled back, "You think I control traffic?" An aggressive fight ensued on the surface. All the while, a vulnerable need was the underlying truth. Later on that evening, Johnny tried to initiate physical intimacy with Lisa, she refused, explaining she had a headache, while silently thinking he was being disrespectful since he had not yet initiated a conversation about what had happened earlier that evening.

Conflicts are generally not what they seem. It is not him, it is not her, but rather often the unseen need of the heart at work. It is never the behaviour, but rather what the behaviour means that matters when you wish to unblock a heart that's blocked. Befriend the nature of your fights; they are communicating something deeper and more vital about the heart of your relationship than you may think. This will really help you to unblock a path to new beginnings.

When we fight, we often think that it is driven by the behaviour, intention, or wrongdoing of the other person. In reality, most fights are actually the deep, and sometimes aggressive, plea of an underlying need that, similar to that of the little child, still remains a longing. Your needs also have a voice with an important story to tell. In the above example, one might say that the couple struggles with a communication problem. Maybe not. The lack of effective communication is only what we see. The reality is one of an underlying blockage in the heart, or the unmet need. The issue is not him, and it's not her; it's the emotional need.

It is never the behaviour, but rather what the behaviour means that really matters.

We all have a fundamental need for intimacy and to safely connect without judgment in love. It is important to discern what is really happening, especially when a need is threatened. She may behave insecurely because she still longs to bypass abandonment with a need to be fully accepted. He may behave withdrawn because he still longs to be affirmed. Effective communication, including listening, is then a tool and a pathway towards clearing the blockage, and seeing and meeting the need in question. This takes intentional work. Regaining the oxygen your relationship needs can be learned by modelling God. *"For the Lord does not see as man sees, for man looks at the outward appearance, but the Lord looks at the heart"* (1 Samuel 16:7). Beyond what you see, do your best to discern what's in the heart and what the heart needs. This builds intimacy.

The truth is, from where it really matters, your innermost being desires to be heard and loved. When it all comes to the surface, the outward fights you see are really an inward plea for affirmation and safety. If there is a lack of awareness and conversation about the need, defensive behaviour that is counter to reviving the heart will continue to be what you see.

We have all had enough fights to be able to track back and see what need was actually screaming from a vulnerable place inside. Because we generally behave in patterns, if you practice giving a voice to that underlying need now, by the next fight you will have already cleared a blockage and increased your heart's capacity in your relationship to love boldly.

Beyond the Behaviour: What the Behaviour Meant

When we get to the proverbial heart of the matter, Lisa's seemingly aggressive approach was really saying, from a more silent place, "I am scared. I need security." She was blocked from expressing bold love by her unmet need. Johnny, hearing the voice of need instead, may have then responded with a close embrace and an "It's okay, I am here with you now." The path of such a fight would then have been changed towards intimacy instead. Then when Johnny initiated physical intimacy and Lisa thought that he was disrespecting the need for conversation, well, would you know that Johnny was actually initiating that conversation through his sacred touch? He is most vulnerable in such a moment. It is never the behaviour, but rather what the behaviour means that matters.

The heart of a good thing mirrors the heart of Jesus. The heart of Jesus is a heart that is touched by our core needs, and He faithfully responds with compassion. *"For we do not have a High Priest who cannot sympathize with our weaknesses, but was in all points tempted as we are, yet without sin"* (Hebrews 4:15).

As you may have noticed, a good relationship requires you to do some intentional counterintuitive things. Even in conflict, when fighting back may come naturally, be intentional to change your response and provide a safe enough space, instead, then ask about the need. This is a really good bypass strategy. Use the strength of listening beyond the surface to the heart, and watch the reconnection happen. Now, that is counterintuitive. But it sure works. Where needs are recognized, affirmed, and met, the heart is revived to full potential. In love, we really do not wrestle with flesh and blood (Ephesians 6:12).

Where needs are recognized, affirmed, and met, the heart is revived to full potential.

Ongoing Practical Application

- When you can't make sense of his or her words or behaviour, do your best to step back for a moment. Step back in thought and stance to intentionally find cues from the voice of what the behaviour really means.

- Ask what the need is for yourself, the other, and your spouse. This will revive a stance of compassion rather than one of attack, and prevent the fight from going further.

- Your heart needs to hear and be heard beneath the surface

Prepare for What Is to Come

"And Joshua said to the people, 'Sanctify yourselves, for tomorrow the LORD will do wonders among you.'"
(Joshua 3:5)

About a year or so before I got married, I was at least spiritually aware that it was the time for this stage of relationship. By what I believe was God's instruction to me then, I began a journey of preparation. I would go to what I called my park of declaration, ever so often. I literally asked God to help me remember those things in my family of origin and culture, spiritual injuries, past relationships stuff, and personal experiences that I needed to discern, investigate, and resolve. I was at least aware that I didn't want anything that was unfaithful to be unwittingly lodged in my heart. I even made some calls from that park and intentionally declared my disconnection from unlawful connections. That was not easy by far. Looking back though, it was worth it all.

I cannot truly say that I was super-mature then or that it was my own wisdom to prepare in such a way for what was to come. What I do know is that I was at least minimally aware of my stuff and wanted the strength that I knew comes from following God's instructions. I now share this wisdom with you. Every relationship that you have had in the past has in some way, or not, prepared you for relationships now and those to come. Discern and investigate any blockages or interruptions and resolve what was, so that you are prepared for what's to come. Make room for new beginnings.

Ongoing Practical Application

- Acknowledge that your heart needs preparation

- Acknowledge what is needed

- Make room for new beginnings by engaging with what's needed

- Your heart needs freedom to love without limits

You Have What it Takes:
His-Story/Her-Story Beyond the Past

While it may not be possible for you to change your his-story or her-story of the past, you have all that it takes to author your his-story or her-story of the future. As mentioned before, sometimes blockages of the past may not be automatically obvious, because they are mostly invisible or seem distant in everyday importance. Discernment and investigation towards new capacity is key.

Unchecked Traditions

There is an adapted Zig Ziglar 1975 story I remember being told that highlights this point well. One day, a girl asked her mother why she always cut the ends of the ham before putting it into the pan. The mother replied, "Oh, I don't know, other than my mom used to do it that way." The little girl then said, "Oh, let's ask Grandma." So off they went to ask Grandma. Grandma replied in much the same way. "Oh, I don't know, other than my mom used to do it that way." Hopeful that Great-grandma would have a meaningful answer, off they went to ask Great-grandma. Great-grandma then replied, "I used to cut the ends of the ham back then because I didn't have a pan big enough to hold it." Ahem, the blockage to a full heartbeat in marriage is sometimes the unchecked, mundane practice of past traditions. Think with me, can you name a few? It is important for every marriage to build a strong enough sense of culture and tradition of its own that is informed but not blindly guided by past customs. Refuse to make the Word of God or relevant instructions for your marriage today of no effect by holding on to unhelpful traditions (Mark 7:11–13).

What's in your heart does matter. It matters what you believe. It matters that your heart has the best capacity to see, taste, smell, hear, and not just touch. It matters that you continue to rediscover who you are called to be and revive your heart and the intended heart of your marriage beyond anything that you may have unwittingly believed. Let's create a distinct pathway to new beginnings in his-story and her-story together.

Ongoing Practical Application

- ❤Think about significant events in your own cultural and family history, and progressively note what comes to mind through each stage of life — childhood, adolescence, young adulthood, and adulthood.

- ❤How, if at all, are marks (strengths and stuff) of such tradition present in the way you do relationship today? Is there any blockage that you need to bypass, or a strength that you need to more boldly live?

- ❤Your heart and the heart of your relationship need their own traditions that are not blindly influenced.

From Expectations to Belief

c————— ♥ —————o

"Jesus said to him, "If you can believe, all things are possible to him who believes" (Mark 9:23)

Misguided expectations often block the importance of belief in relationship and marriage. Imagine saying to your spouse, "I expect you to meet my needs." Now imagine saying, "I believe in your potential to meet my needs." Aha! You got it. This is the expressed difference between expectation and belief. Remember, everything has a voice, and in some ways we all have the capacity to hear what's unsaid or behaved.

A relationship that is driven by misguided expectations, without genuine belief in each other at the core, is often further complicated by the source of such expectations, which is generally unrealistic. While expectations are not outlawed, it is important to know that they often create blockages through inevitable disappointments and resulting withdrawal. There is a ripple effect when misguided expectations remain the focus of your relationship, especially when they remain unmet. This ripple effect often plants a further blockage of bitterness that grows into a plaque of resentment, which then manifests in eventual relational disconnect. All the while, expectations may not even be recognized as the source of the blockage.

Belief is a choice that unblocks the heart, again. It is the ability to see what is possible, as God intended, beyond the current capacity that you see. When you believe in who he or she is from a place of godly revelation, you will affirm this revelation with unconditional love. If he or she knows that in your eyes there is no failure, then he or she will inevitably supersede expectations.

Like Jesus, belief is a principle that moves all of us to take courageous risks, because we know that we are not just simply being judged or evaluated, but also loved. The life force of belief will fuel your heart's expectancy in faith's fullness. This will be a guaranteed anchor in your relationship, which perpetually revives a reality that anything is indeed possible. *"Jesus said to him, 'If you can believe, all things are possible to him who believes'"* (Mark 9:23).

Belief and expectancy tap into more of your ability to focus on his or her God-given potential, even when the present capacity seems limited. Belief says I will love you no matter how you perform. This surely unblocks the heart to a bold reality of love. Think about it, no one is absolutely perfect in behaviour all the time and able to meet every one of your needs, without a glitch. I know I am pushing the envelope a bit, but while this may seem exaggerated, such expectations do exist and are held as valid because of a need that has long been unmet. When you discern that your expectations have truly been a blockage, be intentional to bypass such expectations with belief as your new artery. This will more assuredly revive the heart of your relationship beyond where it has been. *"For we are His workmanship, created in Christ Jesus for good works, which God prepared beforehand that we should walk in them"* (Ephesians 2:10).

Be intentional and embrace every opportunity to say to your spouse, "I believe in you. I believe in your God-given potential." In those moments when conflict looms and such a thought would be the furthest thing from your mind, make this type of response more familiar to your brain. Intentionally practice by repeating this thought and action more often: "I believe in you. I believe in your God-given potential." This repeated thought and action will significantly reduce any blockage of conflict or disappointment, and reignite love instead.

Ongoing Practical Application

- ❤Embrace every opportunity to say to your spouse often, "I believe in you. I believe in your God-given potential"

- ❤Your heart needs belief and needs to share belief

Engage with the "New" in New Beginnings

B e intentionally aware enough to do what is helpful, not just what you've always done. Just recently, I was driving to work in a different car than usual. At one point, traffic came to a complete stop, and I realized that I needed to turn on the windshield wipers, as it was raining and visibility was limited. So, as per usual, I lifted my right hand and pushed the lever on the right. But the wipers did not turn on. Becoming more aware, I realized that I should have turned the switch on my left in this car, instead. Traffic then began to move forward, and so I lifted my foot off the brake, with the intention to move forward as well. To my absolute shock, the car began to move backwards, instead. I know you are feeling this experience with me right now, right? Hang in there.

I then realized that my right hand action had, in fact, put the car in reverse, while all along, behaving as usual, I only wanted to turn the wipers on. My heart throbbed. I acted fast. I pushed the right lever and got back in the right gear to move forward. You see, the same movement that would have worked to help me move forward safely in the usual car was now a destructive move in this new car. To revive new beginnings requires attuned awareness to do what's helpful for your heart.

Do Something Different

It is important to know where you are in time and what is precisely needed to revive and enrich the bold love that God has called you to live. The woman at the well in John 4:1–42 is a great example of embracing the courage to step into the new, even when she had so many reasons to do the usual thing at the well. Jesus' plan for her life in relationship could not be attained until she willingly encountered the new, through Him. Doing the usual, while something else is needed, may be comfortable, but it will also continue to reinforce a build-up of blockages in a heart that truly needs love and the new — living water.

The past is an obscure teacher. Look back, yes, to fully understand the strength of sound principles, and then act swiftly to look forward. *"Do not remember the former things, nor consider the things of old. Behold, I will do a new thing, now it shall spring forth; shall you not know it? I will even make a road in the wilderness and rivers in the desert"* (Isaiah 43:18–21).

Ongoing Practical Application

❤Whenever you recognize the intrusion of then, remind yourself that now isn't then. It is a time of new beginnings

- Literally do something different. Repeat scripture verses that will revive the focus needed to respond differently with what is helpful to move forward

- Think about this particular scripture in your ongoing response: *"Finally, brethren, whatever things are true, whatever things are noble, whatever things are just, whatever things are pure, whatever things are lovely, whatever things are of good report, if there is any virtue and if there is anything praiseworthy – meditate on these things"* (Philippians 4:8)

- You heart needs new beginnings

Strengthen What Remains

♥

Modelling what is good releases more good. I recently had a very insightful conversation with someone who reminded me of a collective reality that I will share with you. She explained that while things are going relatively well in her own marriage, she often feels guilty about sharing the good news, because she is aware that many are experiencing overwhelming negatives in their relationships. Another person said it this way, "There is a tendency to hide our relationships, because we know of people who are struggling, and we feel that we are rubbing it in their faces when we celebrate what we have." So is it that marriage is in crisis, or is it that there are enough good marriages that are silent?

I must highlight that both of the individuals above expressed a strong sense of community. It's that needed gift of "feeling with." At the same time, I believe that a good enough *good thing* model of relationship that is needed is also being ineffectively hidden. So is the glass half-empty or half-full when it comes to the reality of relationship and marriage? Is it that men, women, and marriage are in crisis, or is it that the good enough good news stories are silent, though they exist? When a model of what could be is seen, then a model of what should be is more encouraged.

While considering the strength of community and "feeling with," there is also a great possibility to revive a community by demonstrating a bold-love picture of relationship and marriage. This model needs to be seen. By showing it, we unblock a historical gap of not witnessing a clear picture. Think about it, if history has modelled destructive patterns, if marital relationships continue to face significant strains through a paradigm of maladaptive interruptions, and if unfaithfulness has become an entrenched relational pattern over time, we truly need to see a new picture where and when it exists. When the positive is strong enough, it will effectively challenge and block the negative.

Through my own relationships and therapeutic practice, I have come to learn that there are two key ways to resolve any given concern. One is to focus on the broken pieces, and the other is to strengthen what remains as a pathway to mend those broken pieces. In both processes, the broken pieces are not ignored. Yet strengthening the strength of what remains creates a more sustainable strategy towards restoring what once was or what could be. This is why bypass works. The strategy is to see the strengths that actually exist, and affirm them as leverage towards reviving what more is needed.

We all have a shining star inside. Every relationship has some good to it. When we intentionally focus on the

When we intentionally focus on the strengths, it truly strengthens what remains.

strengths, it truly strengthens what remains. This is the essence of light confounding darkness (John 1:5). Think with me for a moment, can you imagine only acknowledging your spouse's good things for an entire week…ahem…or two, without any mention of negative things? Now, that would really unblock some heart things! In scriptural strength, what if you focused on the fact that we have all sinned, yet God chose to show love by giving us His highest compliment—Himself? Can you see in your mind a list of what you would say for a week or two? Can you imagine what would happen?

We are all called to be a witness by loving like Christ loves His Church. Embrace godly freedom to boldly demonstrate the strength of love where it exists in your relationships and marriage, and enrich a lifeline that attracts your world to desire the heart of a good thing. Let's revive this picture by demonstrating bold love in marriage. As one of my good friend said so well, "We have to be intentional in our marriages to build on the strengths and celebrate them. I am going to be bold about celebrating my marriage with no apologies."

Ongoing Practical Application

♥If you have a good enough good thing, own the greater benefits of being a light in your own world. Strengthen the strengths that remain. Be intentional about magnifying the strengths in your home. Speak about them and compliment them. Then become a street lamp and light a community by giving a loud voice to the good news that could very well model what they need to see. No longer hidden, but rather visibly positioned, with a purpose, to give needed light to those around. This will truly revive the heart of a good thing around you. And, most importantly, it will bring glory to our Father, as we revive clarity in which picture of Christ loving the Church the world sees.

- Be an instrument of scriptural mystery, *"That their hearts may be encouraged, being knit together in love, and attaining to all riches of the full assurance of understanding, to the knowledge of the mystery of God, both of the Father and of Christ, in whom are hidden all the treasures of wisdom and knowledge"* (Colossians 2:2–3). *"This is a great mystery, but I speak concerning Christ and the church"* (Ephesians 5:32).

- Your heart needs to give a voice to all the good things – strengths that remain

An Urgent Need for a Clear Picture of Bold Love:
The Next Generation

c———— ♥ ————ɔ

"Then He spoke to the children of Israel, saying: 'When your children ask their fathers in time to come, saying, 'What are these stones?' then you shall let your children know, saying, 'Israel crossed over this Jordan on dry land'" (Joshua 4:21–22).

"A good man leaves an inheritance to his children's children" (Proverbs 13:22).

It is important to know what generational time we are living in. It is also important to recognize what is needed to sustain what is needed. A significant generational shift has taken place, and this is important to acknowledge. While in the past we may have been okay with "Do it because I said so," this generation will ask you, "Why?" until you are able to produce relevant evidence. The heart of a good thing needs to actively model its character, qualities, and values. It thinks generationally, with a goal to create an intentional path for generations to come. The Bible puts it this way: *"Dedicate your children to God and point them in the way that they should go, and the values they've learned from you will be with them for life"* (Proverbs 22:6 TPT). It is difficult to model what we have not seen. So we have an important duty, in this process of restoration, to model an unblocked new paradigm for a generation that needs to see to believe.

I will demonstrate this through a recent experience we had in our family. One day my husband and I were embracing each other. Just about that time, our ten-year-old daughter was coming down the stairs. When she saw us, she started to back up. I thought to myself, "Where could she have gotten that sense of it not being okay to witness us like this from?" I realized that my husband was having similar thoughts when he asked her to join us. We then intentionally invited her to experience the beauty of this moment, and we called it a group hug. A few days later, we were in the car as a family. At one point, my daughter said, "Daddy, Daddy, could I borrow your phone, please?" Soon after, we realized that she had asked for the phone to take a picture, from her perspective in the backseat, of us holding hands in the front. As she proudly showed us the picture, it was obvious that a seed of normalcy regarding the beauty of physical affection in love had been established. The unblocked flow of love is generational. *"Your kingdom is an everlasting kingdom, and Your dominion endures throughout all generations"* (Psalm 145:13).

I will share with you another recent encounter that spoke deeply to my heart. During the writing of this book, I was particularly focused one day on what I saw in my mind's eye as a disappearing and distorted portrait depicting Christ loving the Church. It was the portrait that was displayed to the world. In this moment, I particularly saw the younger generation searching, with a sense of anxiety, for a clear picture, which was vastly missing in frame. While this discerned imagery was pronounced in my mind, I really wanted to further check with the younger generation. Right then, I was prompted to call a young person. I asked this key question, "When you look around at the picture of marriage that you see, what do you see?" This young person replied, "Trapped, hard work, lack of attention, lack of love, no joy. I get the sense that it is something that I should be avoiding, because it's just an extra burden." To an internal jolting, my heart sank. It is one thing to discern it, but another to confirm it. Oh my.

While from a research perspective one individual could hardly be considered as a sufficient number to project statistical validity, but what if this one voice truly spoke for the next generation? They are truly yearning for a tangible, bold picture of love in marriage but only seeing instead something to be avoided, because such a picture is collectively distorted, blocked, and broken.

It is not just important how we see ourselves, but also vitally important how we are seen by the next generation, who is looking to us for a picture of what they will choose or not as their future. We are, in fact, making the choice for them by how we unblock our hearts to flow with demonstrated bold love. Think about it. Do you know what those around you see when they observe you in relationship and marriage?

Ongoing Practical Application

● Think about the witness you really want to display in love and marriage

● Be intentional about loving boldly

● Make marriage attractive by the strength of the love you express

● Acknowledge that marriage is both a silent and a loud ministry, which has an amazing story of love to share with a wide and attentive audience

● Teachable moments happen every day, engage with them

● Your heart needs to actively participate in the need to restore boldness in love for the next generations to see and then become.

Your Vital Signs

♥

"You are the light of the world. A city that is set on a hill cannot be hidden. Nor do they light a lamp and put it under a basket, but on a lamp stand, and it gives light to all who are in the house. Let your light so shine before men, that they may see your good works and glorify your Father in heaven" (Matthew 5:14–16).

"But the fruit produced by the Holy Spirit within you is divine love in all its varied expressions: joy that overflows, peace that subdues, patience that endures, kindness in action, a life full of virtue, faith that prevails, gentleness of heart, and strength of spirit. Never set the law above these qualities, for they are meant to be limitless." (Galatians 5:22-23 TPT)

The fruit of the Spirit is your vital signs

Avoid Withholding

"Thank you for being just you. Thank you for everything that you do." Does this sound familiar in your world or no? You may have been wired by a cultural reality where affirmation or compliments were scarce, while negative offerings seemed to have had no brakes, even in everyday things like greetings. Psychologically, we are more apt to speak when we think negatively or see a complaint, while at the same time, we are apt to take the obvious positives, in others and even ourselves, for granted. Think about it, how often do you routinely say "Thank you" for everyday things in your relationships or in your marriage? Or how often do you boldly compliment when something is well done. I mean a compliment that is as long as the length of the last complaint. Does the thought occur but stay in your head? When weaknesses are highlighted, without a greater voice for the good things, we actually become increasingly weaker. If you are able to see a positive yet speak mostly of the negative, this is called withholding. Withholding is a blockage that has been culturally ingrained. It is one of the most entrenched cultural abnormal-normal. In a big way, when the alternative to freely speak positives is revived in all of our hearts as needed, it will not only correct blockages in the one who receives but also in the one who gives. *"One person gives freely, yet gains even more; another withholds unduly, but comes to poverty"* (Proverbs 11:24 NIV). Now use the power of your tongue often and speak life, because you can. Then watch what happens to you, and do so again and again. It might be that simple to revolutionize your world.

Contrary to cultural practices, just telling someone how not good they are does not revive their will to change. It more often revives a negative self-concept, instead. The worse we feel about ourselves, the less we produce of ourselves. So even if past life experiences have echoed ongoing negatives, be intentional, do not consciously or unconsciously mirror that voice in your relationship as well.

Incubate Your Heart and Your Relationship

If you are privileged enough to glimpse a good thing in the one you love, or even witness him or her struggling, you have the power to give that heart life-giving oxygen in love. Don't take everyday things for granted. Resist,

If you are able to see a positive yet speak mostly of the negative, this is called withholding.

with every fibre of your being, just giving a voice to things you don't like or withholding genuine compliments about the things that are good. One of the most life-giving things you can do in your relationship, even in times of conflict, is to give him or her a meaningful compliment about the obviously good things. Oh, did you know? If you compliment him or her in the presence of others, it increases the positive heart effect exponentially. Between you and me, try this soon and watch the difference it makes.

Corban

"But you say, 'If a man says to his father or mother, 'Whatever profit you might have received from me is Corban – ' (that is, a gift to God), then you no longer let him do anything for his father or his mother, making the word of God of no effect through your tradition which you have handed down. And many such things you do."
(Mark 7:11–13)

What the Jews were saying here was, What I should have given to you is Corban or is dedicated to God. They, in essence, withheld or avoided giving what was to be exchanged in this relationship by giving it as Corban to God, instead. Have you ever heard someone say, "I'm going to just pray about it," when really what was required was a conversation with their spouse? Have you ever had this experience yourself? It is colloquially said, "Don't be so spiritually minded that you are no earthly good." Avoid withholding or giving as Corban what was actually intended for humans. Yes, dedicate Corban to God in its highest order, but never use your God-focus to avoid the one you love. There are some things you can't just "decree and declare." Beyond the spiritual initiative, it is important that you work at it. Find every opportunity to serve each other, as a true friend would.

Give What You Need

Often, one of the best vital signs that you are growing beyond the moment is when you are able to give just what you need. It is like logically planting a seed of the fruit you want to reap for yourself. Here is the strength. First, if you give it, you know that you have it within you to give. Second, it means that you have the healthy artery needed to bypass in your own heart what has been blocked. Well, that's an awakening. So pause and ask yourself, "What is the thing that has blocked my heart or the heart of my relationship the most?" Is it a lack of trust, a lack of respect, a lack of affirmation, a need for forgiveness, a lack of love? Then give exactly what was blocked. Give some trust, respect, affirmation, forgiveness, or love, and see what happens. Beyond any distraction, including justified blame, fault, judgment, or shame, do your best to give what is needed and revive your heart within and the heart of your relationship with this understanding. *"But the fruit produced by the Holy Spirit within you is divine love in all its varied expressions: joy that overflows, peace that subdues, patience that endures, kindness in action, a life full of virtue, faith that prevails, gentleness of heart, and strength of spirit. Never set the law above these qualities, for they are meant to be limitless"* (Galatians 5:22–23 TPT).

Intentionally increase more vital signs in your heart and in your relationship; it is needed. Life is too short to spend all of your time focusing on the negatives, especially when there is more than enough good to notice in your relationship or marriage. Freeing that compliment or "Thank you" from withholding, and giving naturally where it is needed could very well be what your heart and the heart your relationship has been longing for.

Ongoing Practical Application

❤Speak well of your spouse and relationship

❤Don't take everyday things for granted; say "Thank you" more often

❤Make complimenting a normal way of being, and do it whenever you can in public. Psychologically, the benefits are super multiplied

❤Intentionally move beyond withholding, and speak boldly to the good things that you see. Make this a way of life, even beyond your immediate relationship. For example, if you see someone wearing something nice, don't just think, "I like that." Convert that thought into a compliment. Tell them, "You have a great sense of style." If you see something good on social media, challenge yourself beyond the scroll, and even the like or emoji, to write a compliment. If you think it and it is good, say it

❤To start every conversation with the name of that someone, or with a special sentiment, is one of the greatest compliments you can give every day. Do you remember the last time someone remembered and called you by name after not seeing you for a long time, and how that felt? Try this, next time you write, text, or call someone, start with their name as the first thing. From where it matters, this will make such a difference. Oh, and the next time you are in a fight with your spouse, call him or her that sweet, sentimental name and see what happens

❤Give *Corban* rightfully so, and also give to your relationship what you should

❤Your heart needs to give what you need as a seed to your relationship

Let's make this a bold love revolution. It is possible, and it is needed.

Step 4

ReIgnite

Awaken passion and vision, again, to love beyond limits.
ReIgnite possibilities for new beginnings.

"For with God nothing will be impossible" (Luke 1:37).

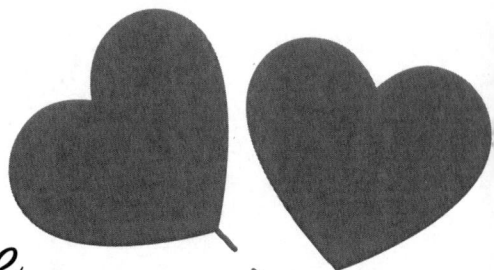

Re*Ignite*
Pathways to Awaken Fully
What Was Intended

c———— ♥ ————ɔ

"He fills my life with good things. My youth is renewed like the eagle's!"(Psalm 103:5)

When we bypass what was, and do our best to revive the instrument of life and love within, new pathways are opened to awaken fully, again, what was intended. To ensure ongoing progress, we are required to reignite foundational principles, through practice, on which to build and rebuild.

To *ReIgnite* means that you awaken passion to stir the heart of a good thing, again, through practice. It is a process that will unlock your intrinsic motivation to step into new beginning possibilities, with a focus on potential far beyond any seeming limits in capacity. Let's open renewed channels for the increasing flow of bold love and good things.

Vision: The Leading Force from Behind

"That the God of our Lord Jesus Christ, the Father of glory, may give to you the spirit of wisdom and revelation in the knowledge of Him, the eyes of your understanding being enlightened; that you may know what is the hope of His calling, what are the riches of the glory of His inheritance in the saints, and what is the exceeding greatness of His power toward us who believe, according to the working of His mighty power" (Ephesians 1:17–19).

I recently met with a couple who were courageously engaged in the process of rebuilding. It was nothing short of amazing how coming back to their long-set-aside vision was acknowledged as the primary factor in reigniting their perspective of what should have been and what was now needed to sustain their relationship. It was obvious that while this vision existed, it was also unaccounted for in practice. Have you ever said to yourself, "I wish I knew then what I know now?" Well, the good news is that now is then for the future to come.

Your Why

Your why is your vision. When this is unclear or forgotten or non-existent, your motion also becomes sluggish; business as usual creeps back in. When your why is clear, however, it will reignite consistent passion like renewed mercy every morning. Clarity of vision will reignite passion, and realized passion engages all of you, again and again.

A Leading Force from Behind

Often when we think of vision, at least in the natural sense, we are aware that our eyes enable us to see. We are also aware that this ability to see is a leading sense for our entire body, with its own why to move us forward. But do you know that far behind the front-row location of your eyes, in the very back of your head, is where you will find the actual centre of vision? Just like the behind-the-scenes son of Jesse, in 1 Samuel 16, the location of your vision, beyond just your sight, is a leading force from behind. Vision goes beyond what your natural eyes can see to include what is revealed.

Vision goes beyond what your natural eyes can see to include what is revealed.

As a spiritual, psychological, and physical principle, it is important to understand that it isn't what you see on the surface but what you see from deep inside that truly matters. This, in fact, should be the source of your everyday why and the driving force in your daily actions.

How Is Your Vision Beyond Your Sight?

If your relationship lacks a clear vision, one that is shaped from deep within, the heart of your relationship will be unwittingly misguided. If you don't already have a vision for your relationship that is deep enough, in statement, to reignite your why, especially when you face tough times, then it is super-important that you carefully consider and create one now.

Create a clear vision statement for your marriage, as well as a family seal, and reference them often. It could be as easy as choosing a particular meaningful scripture and thinking about a fitting symbol. When your vision and your seal are God-given, they will become like biblical arrows that are sent out into your future to perpetually remind you of who you truly are and your full potential to live only in this truth. *"Being confident of this very thing, that He who has begun a good work in you will complete it until the day of Jesus Christ"*(Philippians 1:6).

Vision through Revelation

💜 Humility of heart and a genuine desire to reignite the original intention of God will profoundly change the way you see the purpose of your relationship (Matthew 23:12).

💜 Acknowledge that authentic simplicity of heart is often the greatest soil for the seed of revelation. *"At that time Jesus answered and said, 'I thank You, Father, Lord of heaven and earth, that You have hidden these things from the wise and prudent and have revealed them to babes'"* (Matthew 11:25).

- Be willing. Remain open to the instructions of God. In John 7, Jesus answered the Jews saying, *"If anyone wills to do His will, he shall know concerning the doctrine, whether it is from God [revelation] or whether I speak on My own authority [present natural relationship]"* (John 7:17). Willingness to do the will of God brings increased clarity of revelation.

- Do your best to see your spouse and relationship through the eyes of God. Search the Scriptures to echo what the Word says. What you see in the Word may, in fact, be the behind-the-scenes of what you see right now.

- Knowledge and revelation become increasingly easier to access from a heart that is aware. *"But knowledge is easy to one who has understanding"* (Proverbs 14:6).

- So, just as a reminder, because it's so crucial, if you don't already have a clearly articulated and written vision for your marriage, intentionally create one. This vision will help you to see even invisible possibilities in the future to come. What are you seeing now?

How You See Him Matters/
How You See Her Matters

On our wedding day, I remember walking down the aisle to this all-time handsome gentleman, as I boldly called him my superman in the presence of the crowd. Well, I had only known him naturally for about five months then, but I still see him as my superman even now.

I will let you into a process that holds true. If you are like me, you enjoy creative things. But while I can take a few plastic cups and make a dazzling cupcake stand, I find it incredibly difficult to see a full house from the lines on a new construction development plan. I am relationally wired, but I sometimes struggle to see the full picture through the lines. Am I much different from you? Perhaps we all have, at some point or the other, struggled to apply the principles of revelation and vision when it comes to the one we love. Perhaps you have struggled to truly see the full potential, especially when what you've seen with your eyes is just lines.

To truly reignite passion, vision, and possibilities ongoing, it is important that you make the leap to see beyond the lines of his or her current capacity, and hail the full potential that is undoubtedly within. As early as right now, pause and think about the super-qualities that he or she has. Take a moment to think, then activate your thoughts. Yes, go; you've got this. Send a text, make a phone call, or go in-person and share this super-quality thing that came to mind about her or him (between you and me, you didn't get it from this book ☺).

If your sharing is questioned, don't even flinch, especially if this is not a common practice. Know that any sign of rejection is not a sign of how you are doing in this move, but only their brain trying hard, without immediate success, to find a familiar reference inside to match this truth with. For ongoing practice, here's an intro, "I've been thinking that you are really amazing at_____."

Here is the truth: your thoughts are the igniting fuel for your words. Your words and behaviour then become the engine that awakens new levels of passion and possibilities in your relationship. So use those words and radically change some things that are within your reach.

Your Unique Vantage Point

As a spouse, you have a unique, revelatory, privileged, and trusted vantage point into the heart of your husband or wife. It is so important that you intentionally honour this position. It's a position that no one else can hold or is called to hold. There will even be revelation about him or her that only you are specifically assigned to see. When you truly stand in this unique position, to see into him or her from this vantage point, you will see deep things others don't see and can't see. Think about it, have you ever heard someone say, "She is the greatest woman on Earth," and thinking about your own world you mutter inside, "That's not true." Well, maybe you are both right. This truth is defined by vantage point. It is really a matter of revelation and vantage point by design.

Words from revelation are living water to the soul.

I will share a note with you that I wrote a few

months ago for Lord Dimitri Ngombo Boweya from this revelatory vantage point. It was written from such a privileged vantage point and appropriately shared publicly:

As his wife, I have a unique vantage point. I have a unique call. I carry his fragrance with honour. I am so grateful to God to have been chosen to carry his dimensional seed to life. This gentleman watches over our household so well, and plants divinely given seed in our family. He is the protector of this sacred space. The way he provides reaches far beyond material things. He's a man of great precision. He is a genuine heart. The one I admire in many ways and mostly because of how he truly seeks to mirror Jesus in everyday things. He is the one who fully embraces me, even in those moments when I demonstrate those less-than-fully-me things.

I am beyond eternally grateful to have been in God's package of providential gift to you, Mr. Dimitri Ngombo Boweya. You are such a dream come true — my sacred space, excellent husband, amazing father, lifelong best friend, and my real life superman. Now here's to celebrating and affirming all of God's gifts in you. Your fig tree will bear fruit in all seasons!

Even in those moments when you see the stuff that no one else can see in your spouse, know that even then you are privileged in that vantage point. You are a called friend of God. You are God's trusted one. Honour such a privilege. Resist every temptation to uncover him or her. Stand in your unique position and see him or her with love. Ignite the kind of love that heals and the kind of love that covers many sins. Stuff that is covered with love, not just covered up, eventually becomes a testimony of strengths. As a trusted one, as a friend of God, be passionate about His intended plan for bold love. *"Above* all, constantly echo God's intense love for one another, for love will be a canopy over a multitude of sins" (1 Peter 4:8 TPT).

Find the God-factor in your spouse and relationship, through every experience. I guarantee that in the midst of everything past, present, and to come, doing this will reignite amazing capacity in your relationship to restore favour in the heart of a good thing.

ReIgnite His or Her Intrinsic Motivation

"For I say, through the grace given to me, to everyone who is among you, not to think of himself more highly than he ought to think, but to think soberly, as God has dealt to each one a measure of faith. Having then gifts differing according to the grace that is given to us, let us use them." (Romans12:3, 6)

Intrinsic motivation is the impetus that gets you going, again and again, and causes you to be fully you. Sometimes, through experiences in life or even on an everyday basis, our motivation to move ahead is challenged. Therefore, it is important to reignite, again and again, this needed drive for new beginnings.

Stuff that is covered with love, not just covered up, eventually becomes a testimony of strengths.

Everyone has a great talent or gift. Whether it is obvious to the external eye or not doesn't change the fact that such a gift exists. Sometimes that gift may be dormant and just needs to be reignited. It's there; it only needs motivation into being. It is not only important to know what this gift is but also how to reignite it. Then as Paul reminds us in Romans 12, whatever that gift is, do your best to use it. In marriage, it is an important call for you to seek out this gift not only in yourself but also in your spouse, and motivate it into being.

A Note for Wives

Wife, never underestimate how secretly vulnerable or fragile his sense of achievement, or lack thereof, may be inside apart from what the world may see. Never underestimate how much you can awaken vision, passion, and possibilities in him, again and again, by the words you speak. Your ongoing affirmation fuels his intrinsic motivation. It is often said that a man could have just completed his best work ever, and by far acknowledged a great sense of accomplishment through his impact there, yet in the same day, one negative word from his wife could figuratively snatch his breath away and swiftly destroy him.

If you thought in those moments that such words were simply constructive criticism, well I have been rethinking from this figurative snatch-of-his-breath, unintended effect. So the next time you see from your unique vantage point that he is vulnerably in a great or not so great moment, challenge yourself to strengthen his motivation, instead. Your words of encouragement are like the wind that echoes the voice of God in the valley for him. When said with the right insight, they create a clear view of the mountaintop that is needed, and give an awakening breath where the intrinsic motivation may otherwise have been stifled in that moment.

A Note for Husbands

Husband, intentionally communicate. The minds of women are creative in nature. Women are gifted with the ability to process things emotionally and are process oriented. Your wife may be more prone to having a full-blown internal conversation that fills in the gaps when silence from you is what she receives. You see, that figurative snatch-of-the-breath reality happens to her when silence is what she hears. She then often continues an internal conversation that is more likely to be driven by a human tendency towards a negative perspective. So while you may genuinely need a moment to recharge and ensure that you do no unintended damage, it is also important to know that your absent voice can trigger an elevated intensity in her need to communicate. When you need a moment, strike a balance, instead. If you at least say, "Can we talk about this in a few minutes?" it could mean the difference between a better or worse ending.

In summary, do your best to see the gift and need in each other and motivate it into being. Communicate with insight, knowing the underlying need in the moment.

Affirmation and Security

She speaks with words, he speaks with touch, yet their hearts listen as one.

Affirmation and security are two of the best foundational principles of ultimate intimacy. They are sacred food to the heart in marriage. For him, affirmation is a need. For her, security is a need. For him, it means being respected and appreciated for who he is. It means that who he is, what he does, and what he needs truly matter. It means that he feels adequate and admired in the relationship. For her, it means feeling special and covered in relationship with him, as if she is the only woman in the world. Security to her means that he listens and does his best to understand and empathize with her emotions. It means that he is present.

When a woman is secure and a man is affirmed, the passion of intimacy is altogether wonderfully unblocked. The mystery is that he who is otherwise silent now speaks more and she who is otherwise verbal is now more verbally silent in sacred oneness. Physical intimacy here really means more than sex; it is communication, security, and affirmation at its best. It is connection that speaks in the moment, and way beyond, to the rest of life. It is no wonder the voice of generations is awakened in such moments. Intimacy here epitomizes a seamless union with affirmation and security demonstrated as a boomerang.

Both the woman and man of Proverbs 31 demonstrated this principle so well. I believe that this wife truly hailed her husband as an elder, way before he was known in the gates, and maybe even when she only saw lines. Maybe it really was her gift of praise that made room for him and brought him in the presence of great men like himself. This is a powerful psychological reality in this demonstration. What she praised in him not only reignited his intrinsic motivation to success but also came back to her benefit as well. She is, in kind, deeply hailed for her inner-wealth, worth, and confidence. *"Who can find a virtuous wife? For her worth is far above rubies. The heart of her husband safely trusts her; so he will have no lack of gain. She does him good and not evil all the days of her life. Her husband is known in the gates, when he sits among the elders of the land. Her children rise up and call her blessed; her husband also, and he praises her"* (Proverbs 31:10–12, 23, 28).

The key source of affirmation or security in your life and marriage is important to identify. It goes without saying that for a wife, security should primarily be from her husband and, likewise, for a husband, affirmation should be from his wife. However, without conscious awareness, the primary source is sometimes otherwise. It is important to acknowledge who or what is the primary source of affirmation and security in your life, for this source will also draw more significantly than should be on the heart and time of your relationship. Think far beyond the typical—your primary source of affirmation could be ministry, work, or even a hobby. Be intentional about seeking affirmation or security from your spouse as your primary source, and in a reciprocal connection, offer your heart and time where it first belongs.

Let's borrow these words and keep affirmation and security going, *"Look at you, my dearest darling, you are so lovely! You are beauty itself to me. Your passionate eyes are like gentle doves. My beloved one, both handsome and winsome, you are pleasing beyond words"* (Song of Solomon 1:15–16 TPT).

Step 5

ReStore

ReStore boldness in love, every day, by L.O.V.E. Bring back what was truly intended and needed. Revolutionize your relationships, marriage, and generations to come with a higher standard of bold love.

"Casting down imaginations, and every high thing that exalts itself against the knowledge of God, bringing every thought into captivity to the obedience of Christ" (2 Corinthians 10:5).

Re*Store*
Start, Again and Again,
From the Beginning

❤

"I am the Alpha and the Omega, the Beginning and the End, the First and the Last." (Revelation 22:13)

Have you ever watched a movie and predicted what was going to happen next, then exactly what you thought would happen, happened? Okay, I know that the music leading up to it really helped; and isn't it true that these captivating scenes in movies are never about everyday kinds of things, but rather always about the dramatic turning points that are about to take place?

So let's bring this movie scene to real life. You are now the producer and lead cast member in the *Love Revolution* motion picture. Every step before now has been the leading-up-to-it scene to this turning point. Now, step back and watch your own story and the story of your relationship as it is unfolding. Can you see what's going to happen next? Remember, you are also the producer. If you don't like any part of this movie, if any of it does not speak to who you were created to be, you have the greatest option to start again and continue from *the beginning*.

You really do have all that it takes to shape every scene of your life, your relationships, and your marriage from an *in the beginning* perspective. Use every strength that you have gained, from your heart check-up willingness, rediscovering who you are, reviving your heart, and reigniting passion scenes, leading up to this point right here. So, what's going to happen next?

At the beginning of this book, we started with these words: *Have you ever imagined who you would be if who you were created to be was never interrupted? What if I tell you that you have a limitless source within to fully restore what God intended from the beginning? One step at time, let's intentionally tap into this limitless source within, and live our full potential of bold love in relationship with self, others, and, ultimately, in marriage. The Heart of a Good Thing.* So let's do it.

While practical goal setting says, "Start with the end as your focus," success in your relationship requires that you focus on the *in the beginning* plan of God, instead. You really do have a limitless source within and the ability to change any scene in your life and relationship that goes against who you are and what God intended. In this next scene, you will have the best guaranteed heart of a good thing when you truly take on the producer role to start again and continue from your divine beginning with bold love.

Why Boldness?

Have you ever seen a cup being refilled after it has been emptied? It takes a larger volume of water to fill that cup if you not only want it to be full, but to be full and overflowing. Boldness is the my-cup-runs-over anointing and principle that is biblically prescribed for marriage and relationships today (Psalm 23:5). Boldness is the principle that will usher the everyday signs and wonders that is needed.

Just like the disciples in the Acts of the Apostles when God moved to bring about such amazing new beginnings, your ability today to love with godly boldness will also cause you to leap from the past into the future with incredible possibilities for new beginnings (Acts 4:1-31).

Boldness is your faith's fullness key. It confounds dark things, maladaptive interruptions, and blockages. It eradicates destructive patterns and makes the automatic descent of the past ineffective. Boldness is attractive. It transfers what you do in love to the heart, to the community at large, and to generations to come. Boldness is your demonstrated commitment to live the gift of new beginnings each day by intensifying your love. It is possible. Let's do it.

So whenever you are challenged in relationship beyond today, refuse to reach for any ending before you start again at the beginning. Know who you are and love boldly. Your life in the past was really only "*a shadow of the good things to come, and not the very image of the things [themselves]*" (Colossians 2:17). So rise with boldness every day and literally seek out ways to do relationship with bold love. Start, again and again, from *in the beginning*.

Now, "May God make you like Ephraim and Manasseh. May He cause you to forget the pain of your past, including the pain of your father's house, and may He make you fruitful and prosperous in the future" (Rev. Marva Militia Tyndale, *Recover Your Blessing Birthright)*.

Lead and Revolutionize with L.O.V.E.

The heart of a good thing is a heart that leads by L.O.V.E. Loving boldly means that you intentionally do what is in your power to eradicate every lure towards entrapments. It means that you intentionally raise the intensity of your love standard in every relationship. Do you know that you are a qualified minister of the Gospel? The good news you are called to live and share is love. When you have truly rediscovered who you are to revive and reignite your heart and the heart of your relationship, you are then restored enough to know that the true enemy of this heart is not the person with whom you are in relationship, but rather principalities and darkness. A minister of love refuses to wrestle with flesh and blood. Not only are

Boldness is attractive.

you now aware that everything and everyone has a voice, you are also aware that the voice of every entrapment is the real target of your sword (Ephesians 6:10-18). So boldly take the *"sword of the Spirit, which is the word of God,"* and your warrior blessing as a lion.

Let's do it. Let's L.O.V.E.

L — Leap

O — Over every

V — Voice of

E — Entrapment

Do it, again and again, with bold confidence. Recognize every hidden agenda in every maladaptive interruption, and Leap Over every Voice of Entrapment. You have all that it takes within you to L.O.V.E. *"You see, every child of God overcomes the world, for our faith is the victorious power that triumphs over the world"* (1 John 5:3–4 TPT).

With your own heart and with the heart relationships and marriage that you are in, be resolute to lead with L.O.V.E. ongoing. I can't say this enough: be resolute to Leap Over every Voice of Entrapment. Let's now L.O.V.E. our way into a new beginning revolution. Discern, investigate, eradicate, and, from your God-given identity, L.O.V.E.

God's Word made flesh is perfect. His instructions are proven. He is indeed a shield to all who trust in Him. Declare that this is your reality, *"For by thee I have run through a troop; and by my God have I leaped over a wall"* (Psalm 18:29–31 KJV). Now repeat this often: "I L.O.V.E. to love. I commit to Leap Over every Voice of Entrapment into new beginnings of bold love." As with the art of introducing new options to the filing system of your brain, when you repeat this option often, love's perfection will be established and the interrupted reality will fade away.

May David's declaration in 2 Samuel 22:1–2, 29–34 be an ongoing encouragement to you about the full potential you have within to live this corrective paradigm of bold love in every day to come. Your future HisStory and HerStory in relationship and love will never be the same again.

Praise for God's Deliverance

Then David spoke to the Lord the words of this song, on the day when the Lord had delivered him from the hand of all his enemies, and from the hand of Saul. And he said: The Lord is my rock and my fortress and my deliverer; for You are my lamp, O Lord; The Lord shall enlighten my darkness. For by You I can run against a troop; by my God I can leap over a wall. As for God, His way is perfect; the word of the Lord is proven; He is a shield to all who trust in Him. For who is God, except the Lord? And who is a rock, except our God? God is my strength and power, and He makes my way perfect. He makes my feet like the feet of deer, and sets me on my high places (2 Samuel 22:1–2; 29–34).

Maintain an Uninterrupted Flow of a Good-Thing Anointing

"Behold, how good and how pleasant it is for brethren to dwell together in unity! It is like the precious oil upon the head, running down on the beard, the beard of Aaron, running down on the edge of his garments. It is like the dew of Hermon, descending upon the mountains of Zion; for there the Lord commanded the blessing — life forevermore" (Psalm 133:1–3).

A few years ago, during preparation for The Restoration of Fatherhood, I gained such an amazing insight from Psalm 133 in how it speaks precisely to God's intended position of favour in marriage. It was an incredibly impactful demonstration at the conference and a model to look to in my relationship. The testimonies I have received about how this principle and demonstrated image has elevated alignment and manifested flow of blessings in families have been very encouraging. It's a stance you don't want to miss in your marriage, as you journey to maintain restoration. When you look at Psalm 133 with this revelatory perspective, pay attention to three key points:

1. This Psalm depicts the pouring of a precious anointing oil on the head, with projected generational blessing that flows from the place where it is poured.

2. The flow of oil was uninterrupted

3. While we obviously see Aaron, as named in this scripture, Moses the pourer of the oil remained unseen, yet fully present in his role.

Think with me. Have you ever noticed how much you automatically learn about a husband just from observing or meeting his wife? Ah ha, you are very intuitive. Have you ever thought that you are really seeing him, even though he is naturally absent? In the same way, when we see a pregnant woman, why do we often say congratulatory things to her and not so much to him? In reality, for better or for worse, and when good or not so good, she really shows his glory. When you see her, you are, in fact, seeing him. Here's the truth: because you see the end of a thing doesn't mean it doesn't have a beginning. Because you buy a lone, standing fruit at the grocery store doesn't negate that such a fruit came from a tree that grew from a seed that was first planted. Yet planting the seed was a logically unseen and private thing. Still, with awareness, we know that the unseen tree and farmer is also worth acknowledgement.

"But I want you to know that the head of every man is Christ, the head of woman is man, and the head of Christ is God. Every man praying or prophesying, having his head covered, dishonours his head. But every woman who prays or prophesies with her head uncovered dishonours her head" (1 Corinthians 11:3–5).

When we intentionally live this prescribed position of love in marriage, the flow of favour is also uninterrupted. This is truly how Psalm 133 is manifested. Oh, how good and pleasant it is when a husband stands under Christ, who stands under God. Oh, how good and pleasant it is when his head is perpetually uncovered, because he is meant to remain open in order to receive an uninterrupted flow of anointing from *in the beginning,* and as his wife's covering. Oh, how good and pleasant it is when this oil runs down his beard and covers his wife as she stands under his chin. He is affirmed; she is secure. They are both in full identity through their roles. He covers her from an open head, and her head is now covered by him. She also stands with knees slightly bent, by function, to securely fit under his beard. It is an ultimate sign of affirmation, humility, and her natural position of birthing. So the oil flows from his uncovered head,through his beard to her and from her to generations. This is an incredible, restored picture of Christ loving His Church in reality.

Here's the thing, we mostly see her in this prescribed model of restored relationship because she is positioned under his beard, in front of him. Yet, all the while, the actual channel of this oil of anointing is from his uncovered head.

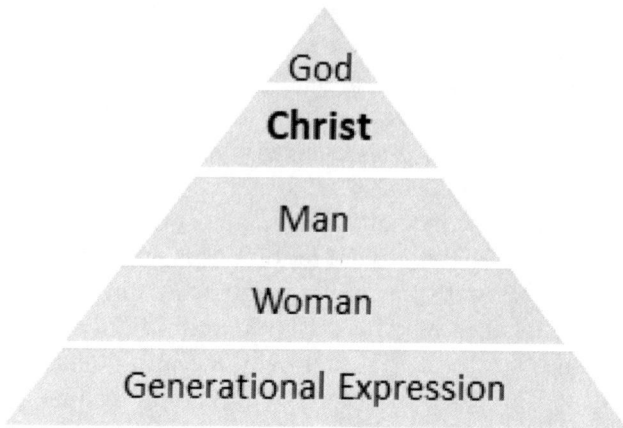

God

Christ

Man

Woman

Generational Expression

Model of Restored Relationship

The message of Psalm 133 is pivotal and continues to be life-changing. As I reflect on my own life, the truth is that my husband is honestly a theological giant. He is a really present father who often makes me say, "Ooh, that's the way it should be!" as I reflect on my own past and what was interrupted. I have a unique vantage point. Really though, I pinch myself sometimes, because I am so humbled and grateful to have seen even glimpses of restoration when it is lived the way he demonstrates it. This is the anointing that I minister from, that is poured from his open head. So if you see precious oil on me, it is really flowing from his head that is open to Christ. I call him my faith-filled coach, because he truly covers me and plants impactful seeds. I am grateful to be his glory.

A note to wives: The seed you carry and deliver is the

very seed that he has privately planted. Acknowledge and honour this reality, especially if you are involved in ministry. For even if he is more silent outwardly or less seen publicly, that seed you carry and deliver through your individual ministry is still the quality of the seed that he has privately planted. For better or for worse, and far beyond what eyes can see, you are the glory and quality of his anointing.

In a culture where men have largely been discredited and women are seen as independent forces, effectively challenging this unfaithful belief system comes from the heart of a good thing. Restore what was intended by being bold in giving credit where it is due. Acknowledge and restore right standing position in marriage as a priority. This will truly open the door for an uninterrupted flow of a good-thing anointing. When his head is open, and the oil of love flows through his beard to cover the head of his wife and every generational seed, the Lord commands a blessing. Now that's a restored bold-love alternative and new beginning beyond a headless and heartless relationship. The model of restored marriage is only interrupted when there is a lack of unity with God's intention for the head, and a failure to see beyond what we see in what oil is actually descending.

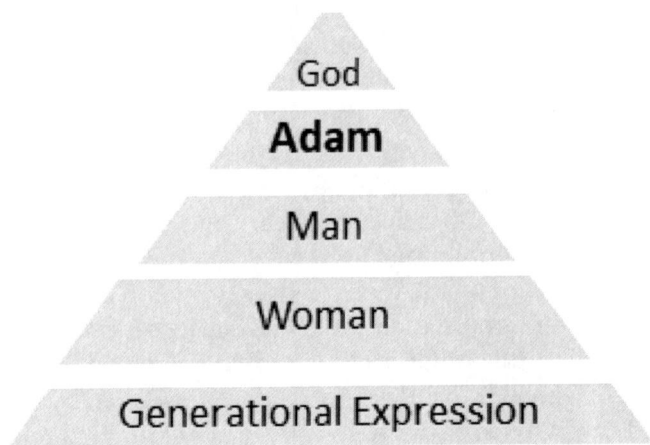

God
Adam
Man
Woman
Generational Expression

Model of Uninterrupted Flow of Anointing

Your ongoing alignment will open the flow of intended favour, both now and for generations to come. Like Mary, when you remain open to the intended alignment of God for marriage, you are guaranteed to manifest an awesome blessing. When you are open and willing to say, *"Let it be unto me according to your Word"* (Luke 1:38), you will find favour in God to restore far beyond what you can imagine through an uninterrupted flow of a good-thing oil of anointing.

Marriage Is a Scared Space

"A garden enclosed is my sister, my spouse, a spring shut up, a fountain sealed."(Song of Solomon 4:12)

Marriage is a sacred space. A sacred space is an enclosed garden. An enclosed garden is the protective hedge around the place where the seed of love and favour is received and planted. Marriage thrives best when she is ordained, aligned, and enclosed. Being sacred and enclosed means that your marriage is protected and that your true fragrance or ministry message can be established untainted. A sacred, protected, and enclosed space is where the heart of marriage blooms and becomes an experience and a ministry that is super-attractive.

I believe that Song of Solomon 4:12 speaks of a wife but also speaks to the sacredness of marriage altogether. Similarly, *"he who finds a wife finds a good thing"* and, together as one, their marriage is a sacred space and an enclosed garden that's a good thing.

Restored greatness in marriage is strongly dependent on your level of revelation and how you practically live the heart of this good thing. The Bible helps us to understand the levels of revelation and practice that should be desired. Among all the prophets, there was none greater than John (Matthew 11:11). He was able to bear witness of the true light so that we might believe. What is striking, however, is that what the other prophets of old only saw from a distance and therefore could only say, *"Thus saith the Lord,"* John now experienced firsthand and boldly declared, *"Behold the Lamb of God,"* (John 1:29). Here it is: what the others were prophesying from a distance, John saw. When you are able to truly see firsthand the depth of God's gift in the heart of your marriage, the quality of your experience and scared space will be highly elevated. Know that what is rightfully far off removed from others in the wife or husband of your youth is actually nigh unto you to see, protect, and enclose.

An Enclosed Garden

If you have noticed urban city gardens, you may have easily recognized a distinction between the most and least invested gardener. One key sign of this distinction is whether such a garden is enclosed or whether it is wide open. How about you? Is your relationship enclosed by God's revelation and your practical responsibility, or is it wide open?

Your marriage is sacred. It is your responsibility to:

- 💜Enclose it by the hedge of the Holy Spirit (Psalm 139:5),

- 💜Lock it through your commitment to a sealed covenant (Matthew 19:6),

- 💜Protect it with the unwavering covering of bold love (1 Peter 4:8).

In this sacred space, regardless of what others think about the wife, she remains admirable in her husband's eyes. He extends security to her. He commends her beauty and her worth. He is present and provides, more than just financially. She continues to be a destined channel of favour to him and their offspring. She carries the seed of favour in him to life. He also remains honourable in her eyes. She believes in him. She respects and honours him. Love is then demonstrated as a beautiful flower and fruit of something sacred.

The goal of every God-ordained relationship is always the relationship.

You see, the goal of every God-ordained relationship is always the relationship. When God's pattern for relationship is planted firmly in your heart and mind, it allows you to create a sacred space, where your spouse can be listened to and received just for who he or she is. This is the heart of a sacred, protected, and enclosed space.

The Fragrance of Your Marriage

Do flowers speak? Well, you only have to ask my aunt, who routinely talks to her flowers and vows that they talk back to her. Really, she is an avid gardener, and in her everyday life she continues to demonstrate an important restoration principle. My aunt is able to hear what her garden needs because she listens far beyond what her outer-ears can hear; she is attentive. As a result, her garden is very attractive and full of fragrance.

Every marriage has a fragrance. This fragrance is practically built over time by how you receive and hold intimate knowledge and experience together with your spouse. The best fragrance comes from a heart that finds safe trust in you, as you extend the same. This is what is then consciously or unconsciously released outwards as your ministry message.

Are you aware of the fragrance you release as a ministry message? What would you like that fragrance to be?

Be intentional and bold about enclosing and protecting the inner courts of your sacred space, and ensure that an intended sweet-smelling savour is what your marriage disseminates.

A Protective Circle of Elders

"Where there is no counsel, the people fall; but in the multitude of counselors there is safety" (Proverbs 11:14).

Whether it's by the nature of our increasingly busy lives, or as a result of accumulative maladaptive interruptions along the way, we are more in need now than ever before of surrounding protection that we once had in community. Do you remember how elders would dance, or actually hop, around certain individuals at church back in the day? It was that moment when you not only knew that someone was being called out but also that someone was there to support them back to full potential. It was discernment in action, with a familiar "Repent and live right" message.

Far beyond the church, Elders demonstrated a genuine role in supporting and counselling individuals, couples, and families in need. It was sometimes not even necessary to reach out, because, like at church, someone would discern or notice that something was wrong and come to surround you. They just knew when something was needed and moved to meet that need. From a place of wisdom and sound doctrine, they would then instruct what to do, and with trust, families would follow through. There was a genuine sense that the elders held our best interest at heart. This is not to say that everything was perfect, but rather to highlight the strengths of a community that was engaged and focused on the wellness of everyone as a collective.

A Community that Secures and Teaches Good Things

Today, the wealth of this type of surrounding community is yet vitally needed. It is the kind of community that allows you to know that if there is ever a need in your marriage, someone is there to genuinely support you as needed. When your inner-gates are consciously or unconsciously down for any reason, a community that is committed to restoring a hedge in the outer-space will enclose your marriage all around you. This is invaluable. Counter to the sweep-it-under-the-carpet, maladapted belief system of the past, recognizing a need to reach out and be supported today is a good thing. Having the appropriate resource to reach out to is a reality that you should intentionally build.

A Model and Reference for Your Community of Elders

This community of elders role is to be the surrounding outer-court and protective hedge around your marriage. Each member of this community is called to stand in a qualified space as an outer-fence. They are there for you with a goal to ensure that your marriage remains rediscovered, revived, reignited, and restored in bold love. They each recognize that marriage is a ministry, and seek to ensure that the picture of Christ loving His church is never unwittingly distorted.

Each member of this surrounding community is an elder according to Titus 1–2. He or she is one who sets in order things that are lacking (Titus 1:5). One who is faithful in his or her own process of relationship (Titus 1:9). He or she holds fast to the faithful Word as was taught (Titus 1:9). He or she is able to exhort and rebuke sharply, through sound doctrine, those who contradict the picture of the Gospel (1:13). He or she is able to speak these things boldly, letting no one despise him or her (Titus 2:15). In summary, an elder is a teacher of good things (Titus 2:3).

The position and role of each member is crucial to understand. Each elder symbolically stands face outward of the inner-court of your marriage. Elders recognize and honour the inner-court as a sacred space. Elders look out for you. They understand that it is inappropriate to turn around, or step into the sacred space of your marriage without invitation. When invited in, whether spiritually or naturally, the tending that they are divinely released to offer reinforces the precise blessing of what God intended. The restorative wealth of this community is invaluable.

Nehemiah's Strategy

Nehemiah's strategy when rebuilding the walls of Jerusalem was a great picture of surrounding, protective community. Though many were involved, each individual worked in proximity to their own place of strength, restoring one section at a time. Each elder in that community had a genuine mind to work, and valued the responsibility to restore the full promise of God beyond what was broken (Nehemiah 4:6).

Like Nehemiah, your community should believe in you, pray alongside you, invest in you, stand with you, seal divine destiny with you, and commit to impacting the next generation together with you. Like Nehemiah, let's now establish a community to rebuild any walls that have been broken. Be intentional to engage whoever you need for whatever you need in order to maintain or rebuild and restore the walls of your marriage relationship.

A Sevenfold Community

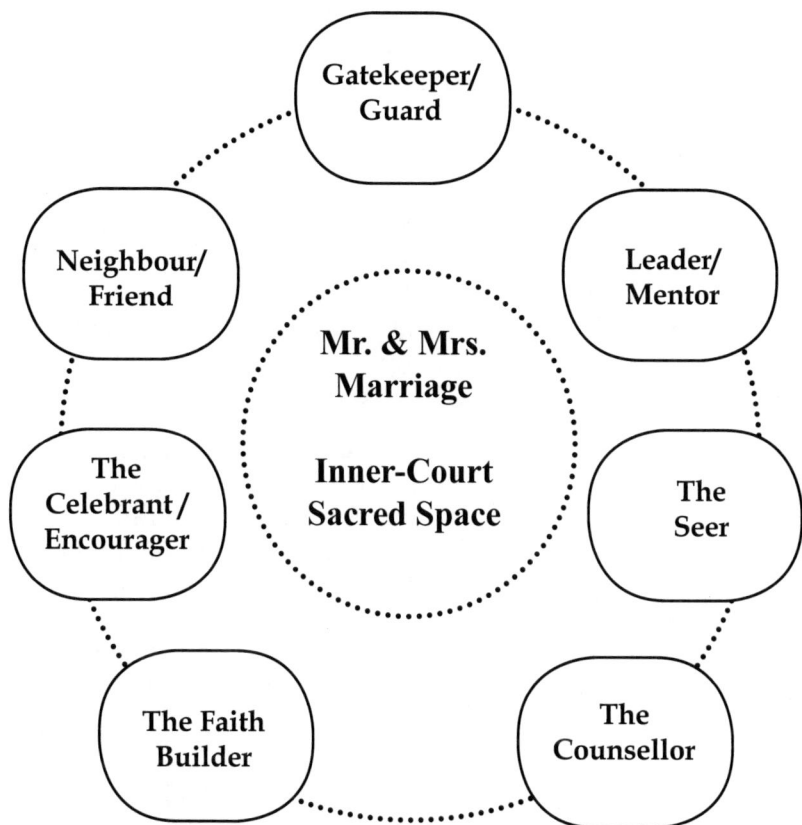

Gatekeeper/
Guard

Neighbour/
Friend

Leader/
Mentor

Mr. & Mrs.
Marriage

Inner-Court
Sacred Space

The
Celebrant /
Encourager

The
Seer

The Faith
Builder

The
Counsellor

1. **The Gatekeeper/Guard (Nehemiah 1:1–20):** The Gatekeeper/Guard is an elder who is a called intercessor. He or she has a spiritually focused role to prevent any further destruction in your relationship, when distress is discerned. He or she supports a continual, spiritual hedge around your marriage, according to the promise, purpose, and revelation of God. A Gatekeeper is fervent in prayer.

2. **The Leader/Mentor (Nehemiah 2:2–7):** The Leader/Mentor is a couple who is instrumental in demonstrating the strength of relationship in their own lives and also in the way they relate to others with compassion. They are instrumental in sharing practical resources with you towards the process of rebuilding in times of maladaptive interruptions and brokenness. They are the marriage godparents.

3. **The Seer (1 Kings 13:1–32):** The Seer is an elder who is called and committed to expressing the truth of God in all current and future projections. Remember, choosing the elder in your community is not about age. Unlike the story of 1 Kings 13, far beyond what seems enticing in the moment, a young elder will hold to God's instruction and will often guide you to break away from traditional things that are discernibly counter to God's original plan for your marriage.

4. **The Counsellor (Proverbs 11:14):** The Counsellor is an elder who supports the heart of your marriage with therapeutic guidance. He or she is qualified to hold your confidence and help you

to overcome maladaptive interruptions through a step-by-step process. He or she sees and helps you to unearth your strengths, beyond any obvious struggle. A counsellor will support you to rebuild an internal space of safety and trust.

5. **The Faith Builder (Hebrews 11:39–40):** The Faith Builder is an elder who commits to refocusing your attention and expectancy on faith that is seen. With New Testament belief, this elder brings words to your hearing to remind you that something better will be made perfect through you. The substance and evidence of things hoped for is and will be seen.

6. **The Celebrant/Encourager (1 Thessalonians 5:16–18):** The Celebrant/Encourager is skillful at practising the discipline of thanksgiving and celebration. He or she will support growth in your relationship, through encouragement. This person will prompt inspiration for celebration and support you in practising this discipline as well. He or she will inspire you to grow even further in confidence, to understand the importance of celebrating everyday and meaningful moments.

7. **The Neighbour/Friend (Proverbs 17:17):** The Neighbour/Friend is one who just loves you. Like Mary and Elizabeth or David and Jonathan, he or she is simply present and commits to being near (Proverbs 27:10). He or she is the kind of friend who sticks closer than a brother (Proverbs 18:24). He or she thanks God for you (Philippians 1:3). Between you, there is a mutual best interest at heart (John 15:15).

Be Intentional: Build Your Surrounding Circle/Community of Elders

Look around in your life right now; there are more than likely individuals who already fit one or more of these seven descriptions of elders. Intentionally invite that person to be an elder in your outer-protective hedge community. It is not uncommon for more than one individual to fit the same elder role or for one individual to fit multiple roles. Establish this elder community with the understanding that it is a needed protective hedge around the sacred space of your marriage. Acknowledge that this community is a crucial resource.

Leaning from Your Need to Where Your Need Is Protected

Whatever your need in marriage is, the relationship currency of the related elder will draw you in his or her direction. With a sound community of elders, your needs have a safe opportunity to never go unnoticed, but to be addressed. Your engagement with this divinely prescribed community will enhance your marriage in ways you did not imagine.

From Familiarity to Honour

"But Jesus said to them, 'A prophet is not without honor except in his own country, among his own relatives, and in his own house'" (Mark 6:4).

Honour is your lifeline to ongoing fruitfulness, not only in your marriage but also in your relationships and beyond. To honour is to actively esteem, respect, and assign value, or add weight to someone, especially to the one you love. It is to treat him or her with respect, not because you agree with everything he or she has done, or because you always count him or her humanly worthy, but because you know and believe that he or she is a gift from God.

Have you ever had the experience of your spouse sharing something with you, with great excitement, that they just learned from an outside source? You listen keenly, thinking "Isn't this the very thing I shared with you before, with nothing near such excitement?" Ooh la la, be encouraged. Even Jesus experienced this reality. Don't judge. It will further reinforce a blockage. Do what's needed, instead.

Honour in Action

Honour is what you do when you bow your highest to become low, because you are focused less on the task and more on the intended blessing. Honour, in fact, commands a blessing of fruitfulness in love. Dishonour robs you of the same (2 Samuel 6:1–23). David and his relationship with Michal is a great example. Even in those times when David participated in tremendously sinful experiences, he maintained a demonstrated expression of honour for God, through transparency, a repentant heart, worship, passion, and praise. This deep sense of demonstrated honour throughout David's life was a gateway for increased elevation and his reproduced reign for generations (2 Samuel 7:11–13). In marriage with Michal, we also see the demonstrated effects of dishonour, in principle, fruitlessness (2 Samuel 6:23).

To honour is to actively esteem, respect, and assign value, or add weight to someone, especially to the one you love.

Beyond Familiarity: Steps to Restoring Honour

Through the following steps, be deliberate about

initiating the move beyond familiarity to demonstrating honour in your relationship. It is a key cornerstone to new beginnings.

Step 1: Like Sarah, who obeyed Abraham and called him her lord (1 Peter 3:6), "in humility consider the other better than yourself" (Philippians 2:3). *Action:* Call him or her by honourable names, then serve him or her according to this honour. It is a sign of affirmation and respect.

Step 2: Honouring your spouse from a pure motive is possible only when you hold a proper perspective of who God is, who you are, and who he or she is as one with you. *If I be lifted up* (the power of the cross), *I will* (increase) *draw all men unto me* (John 12:32). *Action:* Be grateful for everyday things. Don't desire so much what you may be missing at the risk of minimizing what's in your midst.

Step 3: Remember that the benefits of complimenting him or her increase significantly when said in the company of others (1 Thessalonians 1:2–3). *Action*: Compliment him or her often. Use every opportunity to compliment him or her in the presence of others.

Step 4: Moses instructed Aaron, his sons, and the elders saying, *"This is what the LORD has commanded you to do, so that the glory of the LORD may appear to you"* (Leviticus 9:22–24). He then gave precise instructions regarding how the offerings of sacrifice should be made towards atonement for himself and the people. The Bible says that when all the people saw that the glory of God was released upon the altar, they shouted and fell on their faces. In essence, when they saw the manifestation of God, they humbly bowed their highest in His presence. Bowing is a high symbol honour. The humble is then also exalted. *"And whoever exalts himself will be humbled, and he who humbles himself will be exalted"* (Matthew 23:12). Beyond the back aches of the past, when you see the essence of God in your spouse, bowing in honour will come easily. *"And as Peter was coming in, Cornelius met him, and fell down at his feet, and worshipped him"* (Acts 10:25). Cornelius bowed to Peter because God gave him a revelation of who Peter was. *Action:* With understanding, bow symbolically and literally to your spouse, and beyond every "why not," be also supernaturally exalted. *"Enlarge the place of your tent, and let them stretch out the curtains of your dwellings; do not spare; lengthen your cords, and strengthen your stakes"* (Isaiah 54:2).

Celebrate What's in Your Midst

"Let your light so shine before men, that they may see your good works and glorify your Father in heaven" (Matthew 5:16).

A few years ago, we marked our tenth wedding anniversary. We decided to walk the aisle all over again and boldly celebrate what was in our midst. Fortunately for me, the wedding dress I wore ten years before still managed to fit. What a chance. So we created a unique wedding renewal order of service. I then put on that same dress and walked down the aisle, this time with our daughter as a witness, and married that superman in my life all over again. From the feedback of our many guests, it was clear that this renewal ceremony was a fragrance of love and an outward seed of ministry. It was a privileged opportunity for us to be ministers of the Gospel of love. Many mentioned having been inspired by our love to celebrate love in their own lives.

Celebration is a discipline. Celebration is a channel of ministry. Celebration is the mature discipline of everyday honour and affirmation. It is the channel that takes the fragrance of your marriage to the world. It is an important part of your marriage ministry message. Jesus demonstrated the ministry heart of celebration so well. He engaged in celebrations often and established something new each time that became a profound point of making believers. Such celebrations were done with a genuine heart of relationship that inevitably attracted more and more believers to follow along the way (Luke 5:27–29).

Celebration is a seed that bears eventual fruit. As you privately and publicly affirm each other, through celebration, your light of love will be seen and become part of the attractive fragrance that draws others to the strength of what's in their own midst.

Celebration inspires. Believe in the inspiration that you can bring to others by how you demonstrate private and public celebration of marriage. So go ahead and chart an inspiring path for more and more believers through your own celebration of love and the gift of relationships in your midst.

Celebration with praise is one of the greatest gifts and is easy to give. As noted before, look for those things that make your spouse and others unique, and develop the habit of praising them for those special things. If you are married to an individual who is yet to believe, simply celebrate him or her through the Word of God in everyday language and watch the attraction it creates.

Love Boldly

Raise Your Everyday Standard of Love

Recently, I attended a gathering alone. My husband was away on a business trip. Someone in the community came to me and asked, "Where is your lover?" She had such a look of sincerity in her eyes. I then literally paused for a moment to think about the language, and said to her, "You went right to the heart of the matter, eh. Oh, he travelled." We then chuckled together as she again said, "Yes, that's who he is. He is your lover." I was truly fascinated by her boldness.

You see, it would have been quite normal for her to ask me, "Where is your husband?" But to sincerely ask, "Where is your lover?" was demonstrated boldness in the language of love. In that moment, it really did awaken in me thoughts about Mr. Boweya, not just in his role as my husband, but about the heart connection we have. I thought, "That was a great question," and what it awakened in me was beyond the normal; it felt good. I was then reminded of how God works across platforms in His character of oneness to awaken what we need more of. And then I realized how even the translators of the Holy Bible are also in on this oneness. Have you read The Passion Translation Bible yet? It was just published in 2017, and it is a translation that truly goes beyond the normal to highlight bold expressions of passion and love in the Word. That's just incredible.

What we need across every relationship is more bold expressions of love. When our collective love tank has been as deficient as it has been, it requires for us to give more, so that the reality of love can now go far beyond what it was. So are you in on doing more bold love? In and beyond your immediate relationship, do some random act of love every day. Pay for a stranger's coffee if you can, or something of that sort. If you are married, bring your everyday expressions of love up a notch. Be bold. Just do it. Raise your standard of love and revolutionize your world. You are the heart of a good thing, and bold love is you key to unlock new beginnings.

A Charge to You

It is now your charge to love boldly. Revolutionize your relationships, marriage, and generations to come as you live the heart of a good thing. Be willing to have a heart check-up every so often, and be willing to do the work. Then rediscover who you truly are through God's intention, your purpose, role, your strengths, and by resolving your stuff as an important step. Then revive what your heart and the heart of your relationship really needs. As you then reignite passion and vision to live who you are fully, with purpose, restore boldness in love, every day, through L.O.V.E., and bring back what is truly intended and needed.

Determine that nothing will separate you from living the bold love of God in your relationships and marriage. Yes, bypass every maladaptive interruption, destructive pattern, blockage, and entrapment with L.O.V.E. to open new pathways for new beginnings through bold love, again and again.

I bless you now to experience *The Heart of a Good Thing* fully in your relationships and, ultimately, in your marriage. One moment at a time, person at a time, relationship at a time, marriage at a time, it is possible!

"Love never stops loving. It extends beyond the gift of prophecy, which eventually fades away. It is more enduring than tongues, which will one day fall silent. Love remains long after words of knowledge are forgotten. *Our present knowledge and our prophecies are but partial, but when love's perfection arrives, the partial will fade away...there are three things that remain: faith, hope, and love — yet love surpasses them all. So above all else, let love be the beautiful prize for which you run."*
(1 Corinthians 13:8-10; 13 TPT)